WHO ONLY WHISPERS IN THE NIGHT

WHAT
God
Whispers
IN THE
Night

RON MEHL

Multnomah®Publishers *Sisters, Oregon*

WHAT GOD WHISPERS IN THE NIGHT
published by Multnomah Publishers, Inc.

© 1996, 2000 by Ron Mehl

International Standard Book Number: 1-57673-706-3

Cover image by PhotoDisc

Unless otherwise noted, Scripture quotations are from:
The Holy Bible, New King James Version
© 1984 by Thomas Nelson, Inc.

The Holy Bible, New International Version (NIV) ©1973, 1984 by International
Bible Society, used by permission of Zondervan Publishing House

New American Standard Bible (NASB) © 1960, 1977 by the Lockman Foundation

The Holy Bible, King James Version (KJV)
The Living Bible (TLB) © 1971.
Used by permission of Tyndale House Publishers, Inc. All rights reserved.

Multnomah is a trademark of Multnomah Publishers, Inc.
and is registered in the U.S. Patent and Trademark Office.
The colophon is a trademark of Multnomah Publishers, Inc.

Printed in the United States of America.

For information:
Multnomah Publishers, Inc.•Post Office Box 1720•Sisters, Oregon 97759

Library of Congress Cataloging-in-Publication Data
Mehl, Ron.   What God whispers in the night / Ron Mehl.
   p. cm.   Originally published: 1996.   ISBN 1-57673-706-3
   1. God-Love. 2. Spiritual life-Christianity. 3. Consolation. I. Title.
   BT140 .M46 2000   248.8'6–dc21   00-009944

02 03 04 05 06 07 08 — 12 11 10 9 8 7 6 5 4 3 2

To the precious people
I feel humbled to pastor.

For twenty-seven years your love
and care have been a source of great
strength and joy to our family.

CONTENTS

ACKNOWLEDGMENTS

A simple thanks never seems appropriate when people have done so much. I feel as if I should do something special, like buy them a car, build a monument to them, or put them in pictures for all to see. The people listed below have been a great encouragement and blessing to me again and again through the years.

Thanks to the staff at Multnomah Publishers. Every time I visit their offices in the little town of Sisters, I sit and cry—not because they're so mean to me, but because I am always so touched by their tender love for Christ. I never leave there the same.

To Larry Libby, who makes me wonder how I could ever have enjoyed life without his friendship. When I throw bundles of stuff his way, he's able to make sense out of it. He's a renowned editor and bestselling author, so he certainly doesn't need me, but I need him. I'm thankful he doesn't turn down Ron Mehl projects.

I offer special thanks to two scholarly coworkers of mine, Greg Dueker and Keith Reetz, who did a series of word studies that shed light on this subject and had a great impact on the book.

To two of my favorite people, Debbie Matheny and Gayle Potter, who keep my life in order and make our office such a happy and peaceful place to work.

And to the Mehl family: our sons and their wives, Ron and Elizabeth, and Mark and Stephanie, and, of course, our first grandchild, Liesl, whose lives have so profoundly affected mine. And best of all, to my wife, Joyce, who has been married to me for thirty-four years as of June 17, 2000. I know I married way over my head, and I'm glad. I believe that God either loves me, or that He doesn't like Joyce very much. I think it's the former.

"I Am Awake"

Yea, though I walk through the valley of the shadow of death,
I will fear no evil;
For You are with me.

PSALM 23:4

*D*id you ever share a bedroom with a brother or sister?

For sure, it has its advantages and disadvantages. Yes, you have to contend with someone getting into your stuff now and then—and someone else's dirty socks lying around on the floor. But it isn't all bad. Sometimes it feels pretty good having another living, breathing human being around.

Especially at night.

When you hear a strange noise in the hallway (was that a footstep?)...*you're not alone.*

When the wind wails and howls outside your window... *you're not alone.*

When the silent darkness lays heavy on your blankets... *you're not alone.*

When your heart feels desolate and sad, and you long for someone to talk to...*you're not alone.*

And maybe sometime in the night—just because you want

to break the spell of the darkness—you gather your courage and speak out loud.

"You awake?"

In the unlikely event that your sibling really is awake, you may get an answer—something like "Mmmmph?" or "Huh?" If you don't get a response, you try again, a little louder.

"Hey! You AWAKE?"

By that time, your brother or sister might answer, "Well, I sure am *now!*"

The truth is, if you know the Lord, you will never be alone in the dark. He will always be there, always be ready to listen. And you'll never have to wake Him up, because He never sleeps. He's told us so in His Word—just so we'll never worry about it.

"He who keeps you will not slumber," wrote the psalmist. "Behold, He who keeps Israel shall neither slumber nor sleep" (Psalm 121:3–4). David could settle into his blankets with peace in his heart, knowing that the Lord would watch over him through the hours of darkness. "I will both lie down in peace, and sleep," he said. "For You alone, O LORD, make me dwell in safety" (Psalm 4:8). David knew that night shadows were no problem for God.

If I say, "Surely the darkness shall fall on me,"
Even the night shall be light about me;
Indeed, the darkness shall not hide from You,
But the night shines as the day;
The darkness and the light are both alike to You.
(Psalm 139:11–12)

God is awake and alert and aware all night. As I said in an earlier book, He works the night shift, the swing shift, the day shift—every shift! How could it be otherwise? When it's daylight where you are, it's night on the other side of the world, and God has children scattered all over the globe who need

Him around the clock. You may be in the middle of your workday, with sunlight splashing through your windows and the busy hum of activity around you.

But somewhere, it's night. Right now.

Somewhere, a little child feels lonely and afraid in a dark hospital room. Somewhere, a mother weeps into the wee hours of the morning, her heart heavy with anxiety and sorrow. Somewhere, a young soldier walks a dangerous perimeter at pitch-black midnight, staring into the gloom.

So God stays available. He's always on call, always ready to listen, always ready to help. And it isn't like He's there only for 9-1-1 emergency calls. He's there to pass the time with you and keep you company. He never tires of your voice. He's there to talk about the things that concern you, trouble you, puzzle you, excite you.

"I will bless the Lord who counsels me," David wrote; "he gives me wisdom in the night. He tells me what to do. I am always thinking of the Lord; and because he is so near, I never need to stumble or to fall. Heart, body, and soul are filled with joy" (Psalm 16:7–9, TLB).

BUMPS IN THE NIGHT

Why was David so joyful? *Because He is so near.* When you were a child, did you ever have a nightmare so frightening that when you woke up, you couldn't even speak? You tried to call out, "Mom!" or "Dad!" but all that came out was a hoarse croak. Maybe your parents' room was way down the hall—or even downstairs. And the thought of getting up in that hostile darkness (a thousand eyes watching you) and groping your way through the house filled you with terror.

I remember being very sick as a little boy. I had a fever and a queasy stomach. The room seemed to be spinning around me, and I was seeing some strange things climbing out of the darkness over my bed. I remember beginning to cry—very softly. Yet before a single tear had time to touch my

pillow, Mom was in the room with me.

"I'm here, Honey," she said. She sat down by the bed, held my hand, and prayed a simple prayer for my healing and protection. When I fell asleep, she was still holding my hand.

How had she known? How had she come so quickly? It still awes me to think about. Somehow, Mom always seemed to be awake when I needed her. Did she ever sleep? On another occasion I stumbled out into the living room after a terrible nightmare. After all these years, the images from that dream are still imprinted on my memory. But when I walked into the room, dreading the darkness, a lamp was already on. And there was Mom, Bible open in her lap, praying. She simply lifted her arm to me, and as I sat next to her, she pulled me close. As I walked into the room, I had the distinct sense that she had been praying for me. But how had she known? Somehow, love found a way.

David understood that God was very close in the night. He knew that even if he never found his voice, even if he could only whisper God's name from the inner rooms of his heart, the Lord would immediately hear and respond. There is no one more aware than our God—not even my mother! It meant the world to David to know that God was "at his right hand" no matter what he faced and no matter whether it was bright daylight or darkest night. "This I know," he declared, "because God is for me" (Psalm 56:9).

Even in the darkness—even in times of deep anxiety, crushing guilt, and wracking grief—David knew that God was not only awake, but also working on his behalf.

It's a simple fact of life. When you call on God, He hears and answers. "Call upon Me in the day of trouble," He invites us; "I will deliver you" (Psalm 50:15). "The LORD is near to all who call on him, to all who call on him in truth" (Psalm 145:18, NIV).

BUT IT WORKS BOTH WAYS!

There's something else about God being awake all night. Sometimes He has some things to say to *you*—things on His

heart important enough to wake you out of your slumber!

The boy Samuel, sleeping near the Tent of Meeting, heard the voice of the Lord in the night, calling his name. Three times the Lord called him. The third time, Scripture says, "the LORD came and stood and called as at other times, 'Samuel! Samuel!'"

Don't make this Scripture into something weird or bizarre. It's the most normal thing in the world. We serve a personal God who calls us personally and knows us by name. And though He may not speak to us audibly, He desires to communicate with us constantly by His Holy Spirit.

By the third time God called, the old priest Eli had coached young Samuel on how to reply: "Speak, for Your servant hears."

And the Lord did speak. He told the lad some amazing things that were about to happen to the nation. He rolled back the curtain of time and gave Samuel a glimpse into the future. "Behold," the Lord said, "I will do something in Israel at which both ears of everyone who hears it will tingle" (1 Samuel 3:1–11).

When you think about it, Samuel might easily have pulled a pillow over his head when God called. He could have rolled over and gone back to sleep. But he didn't. When the Lord woke him up, he chose to respond. "Say whatever You want to, Lord. Talk as long as You like. I'm all ears." Scripture tells us that God continued to speak to and through Samuel for all the years of his long and fruitful life.

Have you ever awakened from sleep with that strange sense that the Lord wanted to speak to you? Maybe you had a dream that left your heart concerned for someone. Maybe you just woke up with someone's face imprinted on your thoughts. Have you ever thought about *responding* to that prompt instead of immediately trying to return to slumber land?

Not long ago, I sat bolt upright in bed. I had been sound asleep, and in the next instant it was as though I had been awake for eight hours.

I could have sworn someone had called me.

But it wasn't Joyce; she was sound asleep. The boys? No, of course not. Mark and Ron are now grown up and in homes of their own. Who spoke in the middle of the night? Who called me? I found myself whispering, "Lord, what is it? What's Your concern? What's Your desire?"

In the old days, I would have just rolled over and gone back to sleep. I would have chalked it up to the pepperoni pizza or an extremely busy day. No longer. Now I listen for God's assignment. I know that the night can be a vulnerable time and that spiritual warfare doesn't punch a time clock, so I pray for the person He has placed on my heart. If no face comes to mind, I just wait on the Lord for a while, ready to see how the Spirit might impress me to pray.

Most of us are familiar with the deeply encouraging truth that "the Spirit helps us in our weakness. We do not know what we ought to pray, but the Spirit himself intercedes for us with groans that words cannot express" (Romans 8:26, NIV). I'm so thankful for that. I'm so grateful that God can "read" my groans and sighs when I can't even find words to speak.

But do you know what would be really wonderful?

It would be the greatest privilege in the world to so walk with the Lord that I might be able to hear and respond to *His* groans and sighs. Then I would be able to sense His heart regarding an individual or situation and immediately enter into prayer. And I believe that the more I respond, the more He will tap me on the shoulder and move me to pray for those issues on His great heart.

Can't you just hear the voice of Jesus? "What, could you not watch with Me one hour? Watch and pray" (Matthew 26:40–41).

I want to be one who watches with Him.

Yes, I know I can count on *Him* when darkness falls. I know that He's awake and at work for me. I just pray that through the years He might be able to count on me in the night, too.

CHAPTER TWO

"I Am at Work"

W hy don't I just hang around a minute or two, Ron? Make sure you get in okay."

My friend Dick Scott, president of LIFE Bible College, seemed reluctant to pull away from the curb and leave me standing on the dark, Los Angeles sidewalk. We'd just come out of a long meeting and were more than ready to call it a day.

"Are you kidding?" I said. "There's no problem at all. Go get some rest. I'll see you tomorrow."

I waved him off and strolled over to the front gate of my mother-in-law's apartment complex. To tell the truth, Dick's concerns weren't really all that irrational. It was very dark, and no one in L.A. regarded this a safe neighborhood. I guess that's why the apartments were surrounded by a six-foot wrought iron fence. And why the front gate was...locked.

Locked?

Somehow, I hadn't bargained on a locked gate. But hey— how big a problem could that be? There had to be one of those push-button phone box things nearby. (If only it weren't so dark!) Joyce's mom would certainly be home. After all, she was expecting her wonderful son-in-law.

I located the appropriate button, pushed it, and confidently waited to hear my mother-in-law's voice. My biggest concern

was whether or not she had baked chocolate chip cookies for the occasion.

But no familiar voice answered my summons. I pushed again. Still no answer. *Where could she be at this hour? Had she forgotten? Gone out of town? And what in the world was I going to do NOW?*

I sat down on the curb to think about it. In fact, I sat there a long time. Several cars drove by, and I couldn't help wondering what the drivers thought. *There's another human wreck on the sidewalk. Probably drunk or stoned.*

Feeling self-conscious, I decided to walk down the street a few blocks to a gas station. But then I realized that, even if I could remember any appropriate phone numbers, I didn't have so much as two quarters to rub together for a phone call. *What's going on, Lord?* I whispered into the darkness. *Why is this happening?*

He didn't answer right away. In fact, He didn't need to. Dick Scott pulled up beside me just outside the gas station. He rolled down the window and grinned at me. "Need a lift, mister?"

As we drove to a hotel, Dick related what had just happened to him. He had returned to the college and gone to his office to wrap up a few things. But he felt uneasy. "The Lord spoke to me," Dick explained. "He said, 'You'd better go back. Things aren't right with Ron.'"

I had to laugh. It was just one more loving reminder in a long string of reminders. God is at work in the dark. He doesn't go off duty at 5 P.M. or switch heaven's phone system to voice mail.

Can't you just imagine that? *Hello, you have reached the voice mail of the Lord. I'm sorry I'm not available right now. I'm either on another line or away from My desk. If you would please leave a message, I'll get back to you as soon as I can. Thanks for calling, and bless you!*

God is not only awake and alert at night, He's personally manning the phone banks. He takes every call. He's on task. He never

loses track of me, He knows how to direct the resources of heaven to meet my needs, and the darkness doesn't hamper Him at all. You might even conclude that He *prefers* to work in the dark.

A GOD WHO WORKS IN THE DARK

Scripture tells us again and again that we serve a God of light.

- He spoke light into existence.
- He created all the colors of the spectrum, both visible and invisible.
- He dwells in light.
- He walks in light.
- He radiates light.
- He gives light to others.
- He is light.

And one day, not so very long from now, we will live in His light forever. *A kingdom of light.* Dare to let yourself imagine it for a moment! No more darkness, no more night, no more shadows, no more sorrows, sins, or regrets.

Since these things are so, why does this God of resplendent light and beauty do so much work "after hours," when darkness falls? Why does He move and work and plan and speak during those dark times of our lives?

The most natural answer, I suppose, is that *it's never dark to Him.* David tells us that in God's sight, "the night shines as the day" (Psalm 139:12). The darkness and light are both alike to Him. What seems the deepest darkness, mystery, and perplexity to you and me is perfectly clear to the Lord of heaven. Nothing is hidden from Him. Nothing is confusing to Him. Nothing steps out of the shadows to surprise Him. He continues to work because He's *always* at work.

Why does He work in the darkness? Because that's where *we* are! From the very beginning, this God of ours has sought us out where we live. Jesus, the Light of the World, left heaven

to rescue those who were trapped in eternal night. He shone His light into the darkness, John tells us. Jesus was "the true Light which gives light to every man who comes into the world" (John 1:9). God will always work and move and speak in the darkness as long as we have to live in it. Why? Because He loves us and wants to be with us.

Have you ever considered the fact that God works in the dark to hide His actions and strategies from the enemy of our soul? His plans often remain invisible—not only to us, but to the principalities and powers of hell. The apostle Paul explained it like this:

> But we speak the wisdom of God in a mystery, the hidden wisdom which God ordained before the ages for our glory, which none of the rulers of this age knew; for had they known, they would not have crucified the Lord of glory. (1 Corinthians 2:7–8)

God hides His plans and purposes from the powers that would harm us or enslave us, all the while asking His own children to trust that all will be well—that all will work together for our good—while He pursues a sovereign plan cloaked in mystery.

The patriarch Job greatly desired an explanation for his great troubles and sorrows, but he never received one. Instead, he got something even better. God Himself stepped out of the darkness and gave the troubled man a mighty revelation of His person, His power, and His wisdom.

Just recently, on a cold winter morning before sunrise, the Lord opened my own eyes to how He works in those dark seasons of our lives.

PROMISES IN THE NIGHT

I backed the car out of the garage into the predawn Oregon gloom—so dark it might as well have been midnight. Heavy

cloud cover choked off the starlight. I scanned the east, but could detect no softening of the darkness over the bulk of Portland's west hills.

I could really have used a ray or two of sunshine that morning and would have welcomed even just a little light.

Apprehension and uncertainty rode my shoulders as I drove across the Marquam Bridge toward Providence Medical Center. This morning I would begin a new series of treatments for my leukemia. And it had to work. *Something* had to work.

You may have read about my long-running battle with leukemia in one of my earlier books. The form of the disease I have initially responded well to periodic sessions of chemotherapy. While they never ridded me of the renegade cells in my blood stream, the treatments had at least kept them at bay.

But just recently, my illness took an ominous new turn.

Blood tests revealed that the leukemic cells were on the march again. They were overwhelming the normal cells, and chemotherapy wasn't doing a thing to stop it. We tried stronger and stronger chemo, pushing my body to the limit—to no avail. Obviously, all of the chemical warfare being waged within my veins has taken a devastating toll on my physical systems. I've struggled with extreme weariness and bones so sore that just walking around my office feels like a chore sometimes.

Something had to stop the march of those killer cells, or my ministry in Beaverton—and on planet Earth—would be over. My doctors, some of the finest oncologists anywhere, decided to roll out a new, largely untested treatment—something called *monoclonal antibodies*. The doctors cautiously held out some hope for the new approach, but nobody knew for sure how my body would respond.

Nobody but the God who works in the dark.

As I drove to the hospital early that morning, the Lord spoke very clearly to my troubled heart. *Son, remember this. My promises are designed for the darkness.* What a revelation that was

for me! Why hadn't I realized that before? It was for times like these that God had made His promises. It is in the darkness—not the light—when you lean with all your weight on the promises of God!

It doesn't matter what you may be enduring—if you're in sin, if you need healing, if you're confused, if you're hurting, if you've failed, if you're in financial crisis, if you're lonely, or if you've gone far off course in life. In any trial or hardship you might face during your allotted time on earth, God's promises are for you—right where you are in the dark. In fact, *there is no place so dark that a promise of the Lord won't shed light.*

From Adam and Eve on, God's promises have been for men and women struggling to make their way in a fallen world. The Bible's very first promise of a Redeemer came to a man and woman standing among the ruins of a shattered relationship with their Creator. So it has been down through the years, and so it is in the sixty-six books of the Bible. God's promises warn, encourage, challenge, comfort, and hold out hope to those who grope in the darkness.

As I pondered this thought, one of my favorite Bible passages came to mind:

"Who among you fears the LORD?
Who obeys the voice of His Servant?
Who walks in darkness
And has no light?
Let him trust in the name of the LORD
And rely upon his God.
Look, all you who kindle a fire,
Who encircle yourselves with sparks:
Walk in the light of your fire and in the sparks you have kindled—
This you shall have from My hand:
You shall lie down in torment."
(Isaiah 50:10–11)

It may grow very dark in my life before I step out of the shadows into His radiant presence. But no matter what happens, I don't want to make my own light or kindle my own torch in those situations. I want to wait on Him to be my light. As Isaiah wrote, I want to trust in the name of the Lord and rely upon my God.

For now, the leukemia cells are responding to the new treatment. My doctors—and the Mehl family—are feeling relief. But I would never put my hope in something as flimsy and tenuous as a doctor's report or my day-to-day physical health. It can all change in a heartbeat. Our hope is in God. He is awake; He is at work—and I would rather have His promises in the dark than all the lights of Las Vegas.

Whenever I think of hearing God's voice in the dark, I remember the story of hymn writer Fanny Crosby. Although blinded by an incompetent doctor at the age of six weeks, she never became bitter over her condition. She made up her mind early on that she would never allow blindness to darken her life or cause her to complain. One time a preacher, who may have thought he was sympathizing, said to her, "I think it is a great pity that the Master did not give you sight when He showered so many other gifts upon you."

She quickly replied, "Do you know that if at birth I had been able to make one petition, it would have been that I should be born blind?"

"Why?" asked the surprised clergyman.

"Because when I get to heaven, the first face that shall ever gladden my sight will be that of my Savior!"

In later years, she made this observation: "It seemed intended by the blessed providence of God that I should be blind all my life, and I thank Him for the dispensation. If perfect earthly sight were offered me tomorrow, I would not accept it. I might not have sung hymns to the praise of God if I had been distracted by the beautiful and interesting things about me."

Fanny Crosby went on to write over eight thousand hymns,

many beloved to this day. She was not willing to trade away the lessons of faith and trust that she learned in the darkness.

Neither am I.

CHAPTER THREE

"I Am on Watch"

When the one and only grandbaby pays a call on Grandpa and Grandma Mehl, you can bank on the fact that every other interest, occupation, and activity goes right out the window.

There's no watching basketball on TV, no preparing a sermon, no reading a book, no writing a letter, no preparing a Bible study. Are you kidding? Thirteen-month-old Liesl is Queen Bee from the moment she buzzes in that front door. When she's here, Joyce and I just sit and watch her, noting every amazingly cute and precocious thing she does.

Just a few weeks ago, we got to serve her dinner. Afterwards, Joyce, who was cleaning up the dishes in the sink, said, "Just keep an eye on her for a few minutes, would you, Ron?"

Would I ever!

The words were hardly out of Joyce's mouth before Liesl was off on an adventure into the next room, and Grampa Mehl had to shift into high gear. I got up and followed her. She toddled into our bedroom, gave the place a quick once-over and walked out again. From there she peeked into my office. Deciding there must be bigger fish to fry elsewhere, she abandoned that room, too. Continuing her *tour de Mehl,* her little

legs churned down the hallway and into the living room.

I don't think she ever realized that I was hovering nearby. I don't think it even entered her mind that Grampa was watching her every step. Her little heart was full of adventure and the fun of being alive. Joyce had said, "Keep an eye on Liesl," so that's what I was doing. Now someone might say, "Oh, you were only following her because you were afraid she might *break* something—one of your family treasures." And I would reply, "Hey, she *is* the family treasure! I'm a first-time grampa, and I don't care if she breaks everything in the joint."

The reason I watch Liesl is to protect *her,* not the furnishings. After all, she might try to crawl up the stairs and fall over backwards. Quick as a flash, she might poke something harmful into her mouth. She might take a tumble and bump her head on the edge of a coffee table. As long as I'm responsible for that baby's welfare, you can bet I hover like a guardian angel!

While I watched, Liesl surveyed the living room and its contents, then turned on a dime and motored back into the hallway. Anyone could see she was well pleased with herself. A wide, baby-tooth smile lit up her chubby little face. She seemed to be having so much fun. And do you know what? So was I! Cruising around the house in that little gal's wake is a privilege like no other. I never get tired of it.

A thought came to my mind that night as I babysat my granddaughter. It's a thought that has increasingly moved me the more I've considered it. I shared it from the pulpit the following Sunday, and I sensed that others were moved, too.

Here's an old grampa, having the time of his life, walking through the house following his little grandbaby everywhere she goes. He never takes his eyes off that little miss for a single minute. He watches everything she does, notes every step she takes, studies every expression that crosses her face. He tries to anticipate her actions to keep her from harm. He stays as close as he can, not allowing himself to be distracted by other things that compete for his attention.

Don't you think that our Lord treats you and me in the same way?

I have a mental picture of Him following me through my day—going everywhere I go, entering every room I enter, watching over every situation I encounter. Listen, friend, if a poor human grandfather can love and watch over a little bundle of sugar 'n' spice like Grampa Mehl does little Liesl, how much more does God love and watch over you and me!

Why does He watch me constantly? Because He thinks I'm going to make a mistake or break something? No, He keeps His eye on me because He genuinely cares for me. It concerns Him that my feet might take me places where I could get hurt and that my hands might touch things that would harm me.

Please don't think that God could or would be anything less than completely conscious and aware of everything that happens in our lives, minute by minute, through all our days and nights.

DARK PASSAGE

One of my favorite stories in the Gospels is found in Mark 6:45–48. I call it "the dark passage" because it underlines the fact that God keeps watch over our lives even when we're unaware of His scrutiny.

> Immediately He made His disciples get into the boat and go before Him to the other side, to Bethsaida, while He sent the multitude away. And when He had sent them away, He departed to the mountain to pray. (vv. 45–46)

I particularly appreciate Mark's account of this incident, because he includes one key detail the other writers never mention.

> Now when evening came, the boat was in the middle of the sea; and He was alone on the land. Then He saw

them straining at rowing, for the wind was against them.
(vv. 47–48)

Mark tells us that Jesus *saw* His men out on the sea, straining at the oars, rowing hard against the wind. He watched
them during the night as they toiled and struggled in the midst
of the storm. He never took His eyes off of them.

The passage goes on to say that "about the fourth watch of
the night He came to them, walking on the sea" (v. 48). That
was sometime near three in the morning. Was it dark out there
on that stormy night? You'd better believe it! The wild, rushing
clouds would have blotted out moonlight and starlight and the
tiny, lights twinkling on the shore. The sea would have been a
black, seething mass, and the boat was "in the middle of the
sea."

Despair must have weighed heavy on the hearts of those
men toiling at the oars. Have you ever tried to row against the
wind? A friend of mine told me what it was like trying to row a
rubber raft across a lake when the wind was blowing him in
the opposite direction. Talk about heartbreaking work! For
every inch he gained, he seemed to lose two. Finally he gave
up, rowed ashore, deflated his boat, and *walked* all the way
around the lake back to camp.

You may be enduring some life circumstance that feels just
like that night on the Sea of Galilee. You feel overwhelmed and
overmatched. You're rowing as hard as you possibly can, but
you're still going backwards. The skies are dark and stormy,
and who sees you laboring away against the wind? Who hears
your cry of anguish and despair?

The Lord sees.

The Lord hears.

In the darkest times of your life, when you feel swallowed
up by the tempest and surging waves, when it seems as though
there is no help or hope, you need to remember that the Lord
is watching you. He sees you straining against the circum-

stances. He sees the fear that grips you and the despair that threatens to overwhelm you.

And just as He came to His disciples that night, walking an impossible path across the sea, so will He come to you. *If He can walk on water, my friend, there is no set of circumstances that can keep Him from coming to you in your need.*

"MANY OTHER THINGS...."

I've often wondered what John was thinking as he concluded his gospel with these tantalizing words:

> And there are also many other things that Jesus did, which if they were written one by one, I suppose that even the world itself could not contain the books that would be written. (John 21:25)

What was John getting at? What did he mean? Let me suggest one possibility to you: In the dark times, the times when nobody knows, nobody sees, and nobody's aware, God moves in the background of our lives, doing things and providing things that we'll never know about until we get to heaven. Only then will we begin to understand and comprehend all the times He protected us, provided for us, and blessed us.

I've heard people say, "Eternity seems like such a *long* time! What are we going to do there?" (Actually, eternity isn't "time" at all. It's the complete absence of time.) I can't help but think that one of the things we'll be doing is reviewing the moments of our lives on earth and seeing again and again how God was so faithful to us. Maybe that's one of the reasons for all the great rejoicing in heaven! We'll not only witness the unfolding of God's great majesty and grace, but we'll also become aware of the things He did for us when we weren't aware of it. We'll realize afresh that He never stopped watching us in the darkness.

I recently heard about a young woman who made her first

trip to L.A. for a job interview. She had studied the bus schedules, plotted a course for her late afternoon appointment, and had a map in hand. But for all her preparations, she got off the bus at the wrong stop. As the bus roared into the distance, she immediately realized her mistake. This was a very rough looking area, and dusk was already falling. She felt a little frightened. When was the next bus? Where should she go? What should she do?

Some intuitive sense made her turn around, only to see three men approaching—rough-looking, scruffy types. They were walking quickly and aggressively toward her. Gripped with fear, she looked up to heaven and said, "Oh God, please help me!" After that brief prayer, she noticed a fourth man, coming the other way. He was dressed in a sports shirt and slacks and carrying his lunch bucket.

She called to him. "Sir, could you please help me?" He came over to her, and she quickly explained her dilemma.

"This isn't a good place," he said.

"I know. I can see that. Could you possibly help me?"

"Yes," he replied. "I'll escort you to the bus depot. It's not far from here. You'll be safe there."

He walked at her side the three or four blocks to the depot. When they reached their destination, she looked at him and smiled her relief. "Sir, I don't know what would have happened to me if you hadn't come along."

"Well I do," he replied.

Then he looked at her and said very simply, "Euphie, I have to go now. So you be careful." And with that he walked away.

As she watched him go, it dawned on her that he had called her by name—and Euphie isn't exactly a common name! In a wave of awe and gratitude, she realized that God had intervened on her behalf.

I believe that God intervenes more than you and I could ever imagine. Like the apostle John, I believe that if we could put everything down on paper—every time He's helped or

guided or stepped in to protect us—the world wouldn't be able to contain the books that would have to be written.

IF HE'S REALLY WATCHING, THEN....

What would change in your life if you really, truly believed that God ceaselessly watches you? It's absolutely true.

- He enters every room you enter.
- He walks every city sidewalk at your side.
- He shares the office space in your cubicle.
- He attends every class with you.
- He rides shotgun in every car you enter.

He's with you in the doctor's examining room...in the kitchen when you're looking for that midnight snack...in the bathroom as you shave or put on your makeup...in the backyard as you crank up the mower...in the bookstore as you leaf through the magazines.

If we really understood this truth, I can't help but believe that it would change the way we live our lives. If we knew He was watching, we wouldn't want to sin. If we knew He was listening, we wouldn't want to complain. If we knew He was as close as could be, we wouldn't be as likely to feel alone and empty.

Because I believe in His imminent presence, I'll tell you this: I want to walk worthy. Being aware of God's presence has completely altered my life. Now, before I go anywhere, I think, *The Lord knows I'm going there.* Before I say something, I remind myself, *The Lord will consider every word that comes out of my mouth.*

This awareness of His watchful gaze greatly comforts me—but it also cautions me. There is a holy, loving God who takes careful note of everything I do. As Solomon wrote: "For the ways of man are before the eyes of the LORD, and He ponders all his paths" (Proverbs 5:21).

Awareness of God's presence filled Jacob with awe and wonder. He declared, "Surely the LORD is in this place, and I did not know it.... How awesome is this place!" (Genesis 28:16–17). That same awareness made the young man Joseph very, very careful. He told Potiphar's wife, "How then can I do this great wickedness, and sin against God?" (Genesis 39:9). When David grappled with this truth, it filled his heart with song. He wrote:

You know my sitting down and my rising up;
You understand my thought afar off.
You comprehend my path and my lying down,
And are acquainted with all my ways.
(Psalm 139:2–3)

How is He so acquainted with all our ways? Because He's never stopped watching for a single minute! From the time we take shape in the womb and through all of our days, He never loses sight of us.

In the Lord's presence, Peter became bold. He yelled across the churning sea, "Lord, if it is You, command me to come to You on the water" (Matthew 14:28). Then he climbed out of the boat and did something that he would never have dreamed he would do in a hundred years: He walked across the waves.

When you're aware of God's immediate presence, you can do things that you'd never try on your own. How I have cherished His nearness through these days of battling leukemia. Without the daily assurance that He is with me, I don't know how I would make it.

There may come a day when a young woman named Liesl Mehl realizes how intently and faithfully her mother and father and grandpas and grandmas prayed for her and watched over her through all the days she was growing up. If she feels some gratitude and wants to come and give me a big hug or buy me a Snickers bar, that's okay with me. I'll take it—even though I

don't really expect a thank-you. After all, that's just something you do for someone you love with all your heart.

But knowing how things are in this life, Liesl will most likely someday find herself in some dark and unfriendly place far from home and family. On that day her Grampa Mehl may be only a memory, but the One who has watched her every step through all of life will still be right at her side.

Take His hand, sweet Liesl. And you'll never, never be alone.

CHAPTER FOUR

"I See Your Secret Pain"

Can you hear His whisper? Can you hear the love and concern in His voice?

You and I long for such a voice when we find ourselves in times of trouble or sorrow—in the darkest of nights and on days when we wonder if the sun will ever shine again.

And we are deeply encouraged to remember that this is a God with the capacity to feel pain—our pain. He is not a remote deity, some all-powerful being who occupies Himself with cosmic mysteries out in some distant cluster of galaxies. He is not a bored medical specialist who diagnoses our hurts and problems one minute and walks away to drink a cup of coffee and tell a joke the next.

As you read through the life of Jesus in the Gospels, you encounter One who took human suffering and perplexity very, very seriously.

> And Jesus went about all the cities and villages, teaching in their synagogues, preaching the gospel of the kingdom, and healing every sickness and every disease among the people. But when He saw the multitudes, He was moved with compassion for them, because they

were weary and scattered, like sheep having no shepherd. (Matthew 9:35–36)

He sat on a hillside with His disciples, watching crowds of people wind their way toward Him. His eyes scanned the multitude, and those sitting closest to Him must have heard Him sigh.

But did they know why He sighed so deeply?

The disciples, after all, saw only crowds. Jesus saw people.

The disciples were probably amazed by the sheer number of people who sought out the Master. They saw a great throng—perhaps an unpredictable mob, but surely a massive logistics problem. Jesus saw individual men, women, boys, and girls.

The disciples saw people as they were at the moment, trudging up a hillside in the morning sunlight. Jesus saw life histories.

What sort of people did He see? He saw the blind, the disabled, and the poor. He saw the wealthy, the prominent, and the influential. He saw leaders and followers, husbands and wives, fathers and sons, mothers and daughters. He saw people who had edged very near the kingdom of God—right up to the threshold—and others who had come out of curiosity rather than conviction. He saw lives that were in darkness, even in the middle of the day.

If you and I had been seated with Jesus that day, looking out across the crowds, we might have seen evidence of unhappiness or worry here and there. A woman's slumping shoulders. A young child's cry. An old man's heavy shuffle. A frown. A shake of the head. But the Son of David saw more than that. He saw into the depths of minds and hearts. He saw abandoned dreams and withered hopes and hurts so deep they could hardly be plumbed.

Scripture says that He saw men and women who were weary, broken, and harassed. He saw people who were direc-

tionless and helpless, like sheep chased by predators, with no shepherd to protect or guide them.

Outwardly, many of them may have appeared successful and satisfied. But "the LORD does not see as man sees; for man looks at the outward appearance, but the LORD looks at the heart" (1 Samuel 16:7). He saw their hearts and felt the emptiness, the distress, the worry, the anxiety. He felt the awful ache of loneliness, weariness, and discouragement that dragged on their spirits like an anchor. And He was moved with compassion by the needs of each soul.

That's the way Jesus always saw:

- He saw the rich young ruler and loved him. He saw exactly what was holding back that earnest young man from stepping into eternal life.
- He saw the woman at the well not as a Samaritan, a foreigner, or an adulteress. He saw her thirst, which went much deeper than a craving for water or fleeting relationships with men.
- He saw His dear friend Martha, who always seemed so in control, and knew that inwardly she was "worried and troubled about many things."
- He saw Zacchaeus, a despised tax gatherer, scorned as a cheat and a Roman collaborator. He saw the little man's deep weariness with life, his overwhelming desire to escape the pit he'd dug for himself, and a flickering hunger for God ready to burst into flame.

Jesus is just the same today. He still sees. When John saw the resurrected Christ in all His glory—the way He appears in heaven right now—it was natural for the apostle to seek out the eyes of his old friend and teacher. But how startling those eyes must have been! John wrote, "His eyes [were] like a flame of fire" (Revelation 1:14).

Those are eyes you cannot fool. No one pulls the wool over

those eyes—eyes that burn through all of our masks and masquerades...eyes that see motives beneath actions...eyes that discern sorrow beneath empty laughter...eyes that pierce to the depths of our souls.

NEGATIVE IMAGES

Not long ago, I got a call from Paul, a close friend of mine who is a pastor in another state. I knew immediately that something was wrong. His normally buoyant voice sounded broken and strained.

His daughter, Kelly, a freshman at a big university, had just come home for spring break. It had been such fun to have her back and to have the whole family together again.

One afternoon while Kelly was out with some friends, Paul felt moved to do something "fatherly" for his girl. He would clean up her car, get it washed and waxed, and then take it for an oil change and lube.

As he was vacuuming the seats, he saw something wedged between the seat and the console. An ID card. He didn't recognize the name on the card, but the picture looked familiar. Then it hit him. This was one of Kelly's older friends, who happened to look a lot like his daughter. Why would Kelly have such an ID card in her possession? Unless....

A ripple of ice water went through Paul's veins.

Alongside the ID card he found a ticket stub to a movie, the kind of movie he never imagined his daughter watching—or even wanting to watch.

Right after that, he found a roll of undeveloped film.

And that presented him with a dilemma. Kelly had always been an ideal daughter. Loving. Trustworthy. Obedient. She had been an active member of their church and its youth group when she was growing up and had never given her parents a day of trouble in her life. So naturally Paul wanted to think the best. The ID and ticket stub, after all, might be explained away. They might belong to one of her friends. *But what would the film*

reveal? Should he find out? It would be an intrusion, and yet....

He thought, *Lord, forgive me if this is wrong. But in case there's something on this film that will help me understand what's going on in Kelly's life, I'm going to develop it.*

After Kelly had returned to college, Paul got the pictures back and looked through them. One in particular disturbed him deeply. It was a picture of Kelly lounging in a big beanbag chair with a bottle of beer in one hand and a cigarette in the other. She was surrounded by a group of guys—the kind that a father doesn't want his daughter surrounded by.

Heartbroken, Paul sat with the pictures in his lap and his face buried in his hands. So…all of that aura of normality—that simple joy of being home and resuming the old activities—had been a sham. Something manufactured. That really hurt. What bothered him most about the photograph wasn't the beer or the cigarette. It wasn't anything he could physically see in the picture. It was Kelly's apparent attitude. It was the ease with which she sat there, doing what she was doing.

She looked very comfortable in that setting.

How could this happen? Why would she do this?

He showed the pictures to his wife, Angie, and after discussing the situation, they decided that Paul needed to drive to Kelly's apartment at school and talk with her face-to-face.

He rang the bell, and Kelly opened the door. She was so shocked that for a moment she couldn't speak. Finally she said, "What are *you* doing here?"

"I need to talk to you," he told her. "Can you come for a drive with me?"

They drove in silence, Kelly confused and apprehensive, Paul uncertain how to open the conversation. They ended up in the parking lot of a little church, under a streetlight. Paul wanted light in the car so he could see Kelly's face.

"I was cleaning your car while you were home," he began, "and I found some things." He showed her the picture.

"Honey," he said, "is there anything in this picture that you think might break your father's heart?"

Kelly took the picture, looked at it in silence for a moment, and handed it back. "Yes," she answered.

He wasn't really sure what he had been hoping for in that moment. Some tenderness maybe? Some remorse? A few tears? Yet when she looked at him, her eyes were dry. She seemed hard. Cold.

"You know, Kelly," he said to her, "when you step over the line and extend your borders, you'll keep pushing beyond the things you once believed and stood for."

He started the car and handed her the picture. "Here," he said. "You take this. Go back to your apartment and put it up on your mirror. Every morning when you get up, look at it and ask yourself, 'Is this what God made me to be?'"

Paul wept as he parted with Kelly at the apartment. Everything wasn't fine; everything wasn't fixed. He embraced her, and she was limp as a doll. There was no embrace in return.

Both Paul and Angie grieved. For days, Angie cried herself to sleep at night. These were the darkest times they had ever experienced as a family. All they could do was keep coming before the Lord in prayer, trusting in His care and faithfulness.

You and I never *really* know what's in a person's heart, do we? We can't always see the darkness—the long shadows of pain and worry. When the people in my friend's congregation greeted their pastor and his wife at the front door of the church, they didn't have any idea that Paul and Angie's hearts were breaking. And Paul and Angie hadn't had a clue that their daughter was leading a very different sort of life at college than she had lived at home.

They didn't see until the film was developed.

But the Lord sees the undeveloped film. His eyes see into film canisters—and deeper still. His eyes see every corner of the heart.

For my friends, there was a happy ending. Several days later, Kelly showed up at home. She had seen how deeply she had wounded her parents, and the Lord had worked on her heart. She told them she had been wrong and how sorry she was for causing so much pain. She's still in college, but now she's studying with a purpose. She wants to prepare herself to serve the Lord.

Does your life seem dark today? Do you have hurts that others can't see? Wounds you can't even put into words? Aches that are years deep and reach into the back rooms of your soul?

Be assured one thing, friend. As dark as it may seem, BE VERY, VERY SURE OF THIS:

The Son of God sees.

And He is moved with compassion by what He sees.

A Feeling in the Gut

Within the New Testament word for compassion is the term *bowels*. Both the Greeks and Hebrews felt that deep emotions originated in the bowels, or intestines. That isn't so very strange, is it? After all, we might say, "I have a gut feeling about this" or "He felt it in his gut." And I don't think it would be inaccurate or irreverent to say that the Lord Jesus *felt in His gut* what He saw in troubled hearts.

And—whether you've realized it or not, whether you believe it or not—the mighty Son of God is moved by *your* troubled heart.

Don't ask me to explain it, because I can't. I can only tell you that the Bible says it is so. David had trouble comprehending it, too. Shaking his head in wonder, he wrote:

O LORD, You have searched me and known me.
You know my sitting down and my rising up;
You understand my thought afar off.
You comprehend my path and my lying down,
And are acquainted with all my ways.

For there is not a word on my tongue,
But behold, O LORD, You know it altogether.
You have hedged me behind and before,
And laid Your hand upon me.
Such knowledge is too wonderful for me;
It is high, I cannot attain it.
(Psalm 139:1–6)

We say with David, "How could this be? How could He see me and know me like that? How could He listen in on my thoughts? How could He know my troubled heart? I can't comprehend a God so vast and powerful!"

You and I can't know what's going on inside those around us. Our eyes can't see beneath the reserved expressions and the carefully kept exteriors. We can't even begin to see what people have endured or are enduring.

I think of my dear friends Chuck and Lorna Bradley, members of our church in Beaverton and one of the most impressive, loving, and physically striking couples I have ever met. Chuck is a former Miami Dolphin. He was the number-one draft choice coming out of the University of Oregon, and in his very first year in the league, his team won the Super Bowl. He stands six-foot-six and has the broad shoulders and muscular physique of a man who still looks ready to step onto the gridiron. Lorna, a truly beautiful woman as well as a gifted singer and musician, graces the piano bench during our worship services. You could look at them and think to yourself, *No couple should look that nice this side of heaven. No two people should have such sweet spirits.*

To watch them walk into church on a Sunday morning, you'd think that they couldn't have a trouble in the world. You would never guess the agony they've been through. But the Lord sees beyond the physical beauty and the outward signs of success. The Lord has seen and felt their long, long night of pain.

When their son Landon was two years old, he was struck by a car and critically injured. The first thing that went through Chuck Bradley's mind after the accident was, *Who missed his assignment? Who messed up? Who did it wrong?*

It was a knee-jerk reaction for a former NFL starting center, because whenever a quarterback gets sacked or a running back gets stuffed, somebody on the offensive line is in trouble. Count on it. The first thing the quarterback, head coach, offensive coach, running back, and about nine million fans want to know is: *Who missed his assignment?*

More often than not, a player's number comes up. The television cameras zoom in on the guilty party, and the mistake is played over and over again in slow motion. Number 52 missed a block. He didn't even slow down that nose tackle. He didn't fill the gap. That's why that fragile, multimillion-dollar quarterback was leveled like he'd been hit by a freight train.

Chuck knew all about taking heat for a missed assignment. As the center for the world-champion Dolphins, he was well aware of the need to protect the legendary Bob Griese and give him time to find the equally legendary Paul Warfield downfield.

So why couldn't he protect his little boy? Why hadn't he been there to stand in the gap when the car came around the corner?

When Landon died of his injuries a few days later, Chuck felt as though someone was screaming his number. Somehow, in some way, it must have happened because of a fault in his life. Somehow he must have been responsible!

In his five-year pro career, Chuck had been on the receiving end of some unbelievably powerful hits. He had been blindsided, steamrolled, and scissored. He'd been injured and knocked unconscious. Most of the time, he'd been able to pick himself up, dust himself off, and go back to the huddle or hobble over to the sideline.

But no hit in all his life had ever hurt like this one. He

couldn't stop blaming himself. And the hurt didn't fade with the passing of days. It grew harder and harder to bear.

Lorna hurt just as much. She had been there when it happened. She saw it all. The scene was imprinted on her mind in all its horror. Whenever she closed her eyes, she saw it. For weeks afterward, she was afraid to go to bed at night because she couldn't bear to see the tragedy replayed, over and over again.

The days were long and dark, and the nights were even worse. What do you do with that kind of grief? Where do you go? Where do you turn? Well-meaning people told them to lean on old friends, read books, take long trips, or sit in on therapy groups. But those things don't help that kind of pain. You can't bury it with words. And how could anyone really identify with such a loss? How could anyone really understand such pain? So deep! So constant!

In the end, Chuck and Lorna heard a whisper in the night.

They learned that only One could reach deep enough into their troubled hearts to touch them and bring healing. People were kind and sympathetic, but only Jesus could see, feel, and understand.

What does it mean to you and me that Jesus Christ can see into our hearts and speak a word into our darkest hours?

- It means that there is One who is with us in our pain. *We cannot say we are alone.*
- It means that there is One who truly sees and comprehends what we are going through and knows the true source of our distress. *We cannot say no one understands.*
- It means that there is One who feels the intensity of our hurts and is moved with compassion toward us. *We cannot say no one cares.*

In the pages that follow, we will learn to listen for the voice that whispers to us in the dark. Much of the time, we'll walk

with King David, who so freely expressed the deep-rooted emotions of his heart, letting them spill out across the pages of the Psalms.

Remember, you may find yourself in the darkness, but you will never find yourself alone. God is there, and He is wide-awake. He sees the old wounds and fresh hurts better than you see them yourself.

That's what He's whispering to you, right now.

CHAPTER FIVE

"Don't Worry"

King David struggled with worry and anxiety for years. As an old man, he offered his counsel on where to turn when the dark times come. "I have been young," he wrote in Psalm 37, "and now am old...." (Psalm 37:25).

As I read this psalm, I picture myself walking through the palace gardens at twilight with old King David. As we stroll together down the palm-lined pathways in the cool fragrance of a Jerusalem evening, he clasps his hands behind his back. The wind billows his robe and ruffles his hair and flowing silver beard. He gazes at the horizon as he speaks, watching the first stars wink in the sky, just as he had watched them as a shepherd boy so many years before.

When he turns to look at me, his eyes are full of wisdom. These are eyes that have seen great pain, loneliness, disappointment, and grief...but they have also seen beyond the pressures and shadows of daily life.

This is a man who has heard God's whisper in the night.

This is a man who has sustained his life on the promises of God.

Psalm 37 is what students of the Bible call a "wisdom

psalm." And isn't that what we need when our lives seem confused, when circumstances seem out of control, when our mind feels weary, and when our hearts are aching? Just a little quiet wisdom and comfort from someone we can trust.

COUNSEL YOU CAN DEPEND ON

Sometimes people offer counsel right off the top of their heads. Their words are thoughtless and have no depth. They are words you can't depend on, for they have neither substance nor root.

When I was first diagnosed with leukemia, people would say the strangest things to me. They would make offhand speculations about possible sins in my life, remark about my lack of faith, or take me aside to share some bizarre cure they had heard about from a great aunt in Delaware. Already struggling with worry, I wasn't helped or comforted at all by their "counsel." It would have been better had they just said they would pray for me—or said nothing at all.

But David's counsel isn't like that. His words are never trite or thoughtless. His words are not only drawn out of a deep well of personal experience, they are also inspired by the living God. David had walked with the Lord as a simple shepherd boy and learned about his God through long, silent days and nights out in the fields. He had learned from the Lord through the hard, lean years as a young man on the run, a lonely fugitive with a price on his head.

As we walk, David wants to tell me the things he has learned. He has counsel for me to follow. But before he tells me what I ought to do, he stops in the path and lays a weathered hand on my shoulder. Before anything else, he tells me what *not* to do.

"Son," he says gently, "don't fret yourself."

When we hear the word *fret,* we usually think of worry in general. But David has something more specific in mind here. In Psalm 37, David says that comparison and envy make our hearts anxious. When we take our eyes off the Lord, off

heaven, off His provision, off His promises, we become worried and upset. Anger builds, frustration boils, and we begin to question God's goodness toward us and even wonder if He really loves us at all.

The psalm begins with counsel for people who find themselves at the short end of the stick more times than they would care to count—and are just about fed up with it. David is speaking to people who are trying to cling to God's Word and God's ways in life but keep getting cut off by people taking shortcuts—people who care nothing for God or anyone but themselves.

Through the words of his psalm, David gently urges us to have a different perspective—a long view of life, instead of a short one. But it isn't easy....

MIKE'S LEGACY

Not long ago, I attended the funeral of a dear friend named Mike. Mike was only fifty-three when he passed away. For years he had been a faithful pastor in a small-town church that could never seem to climb over the 100 mark in attendance. He studied hard and poured himself into his sermons. Like an alert shepherd, he made himself available night and day, visiting the sick, encouraging the weak, and giving himself away.

When someone faced a moving day, Mike showed up to pack boxes. When someone needed help digging an irrigation ditch, Mike was on site with his work gloves and shovel. Anything to help. Anything to encourage. Anything to shepherd. Anything to show the love of Jesus.

But despite all his efforts, the church didn't grow. Little by little, for one reason and another, attendance dropped. When the depleted congregation could no longer support them, he and his wife began managing a small inn. So in addition to pastoral visitations and studying for sermons, he found himself cleaning rooms, doing maintenance, balancing the books, and answering the telephone.

It was a lot to handle. In fact, it was too much. One night Mike died in bed of a massive heart attack.

I attended his memorial service in the tiny funeral chapel. It was a small gathering: some folks from the church; a few people from the community where he had poured out his life; his wife and kids; Joyce and I. There were no denominational leaders or people of renown and only a couple of sprays of flowers.

People might say that Mike hadn't made a very big splash on the ministry scene. He was never on radio or television or written up in a magazine. He never had a column in the newspaper, and he never wrote a book.

He just loved his family and gave himself for his little flock. In some people's eyes, that didn't merit much attention. In other people's eyes, it spelled failure. But as I stood there, I realized how much richer my life was because of Mike. His priorities were right: God, family, and ministry.

That night I went back to my motel room and wept.

It didn't seem fair or right. He was a better man than I'll ever be, and from the world's point of view, he ended up with nothing. If you think about it long enough, it's enough to make you angry or even a little bitter. It's enough to keep you awake at night.

But David says, "Don't let that happen, friend. Don't get caught playing the comparison game." Mike didn't. Oh sure, just like any of us, he probably became frustrated or discouraged now and then. That's part of the tuition we pay for being human. But Mike's focus in life was locked on something beyond daily circumstances—no matter how pressing and distressing. Mike focused on the promises of God.

Mike understood that God rewards faithfulness—not fruitfulness—and that He knows very well how to reward His servants in His time. I think Mike must have learned what David had learned in the long, bitter years of running and hiding in the wilderness—that life can be lived on two levels.

LIFE ON TWO LEVELS

On one level, present circumstances press in from all sides. As a young man, David's circumstances were anything but pleasant. Oh, yes, he had the promise of kingship. God's prophet had poured the oil of anointing on his head, and David knew there was a promised throne out there—somewhere. In the meantime, however...

> he was lonely;
> he was hungry and thirsty;
> he was in danger;
> he was afraid;
> he was weary;
> he was heavy hearted;
> he was separated from friends and family.

From his hiding places, he could no doubt look out at the camps of the soldiers who were hounding him. He could smell meat roasting over bright, crackling fires. His enemies were warm. They had food and drink and adequate clothing. They told stories and laughed around the campfire. They could go home to their wives and bounce their little ones on their knees. They were relaxed. They enjoyed job security.

David might have been tempted to think, *Just who is living like a king around here? Not me, that's for sure! This is a terrible life! It isn't right. It isn't fair.*

It must have been on one of those dark, lonely nights when he wrote these words:

> My eye wastes away with grief,
> Yes, my soul and my body!
> For my life is spent with grief,
> And my years with sighing....
> I am a reproach among all my enemies,

But especially among my neighbors,
And am repulsive to my acquaintances;
Those who see me outside flee from me.
I am forgotten like a dead man, out of mind;
I am like a broken vessel.
(Psalm 31:9–12)

That was one level of life. But there was another, and again and again that's where David chose to live—at the level of the promises of God. Through most of his psalms, you hear David moving from a focus on his present, painful circumstances toward a focus on the person, promises, and provision of God.

Listen....

For I hear the slander of many;
Fear is on every side;
While they take counsel together against me,
They scheme to take away my life.

But as for me, I trust in You, O LORD;
I say, "You are My God."
My times are in Your hand....

Oh, how great is Your goodness,
Which You have laid up for those who fear You,
Which You have prepared for those who trust in You.
(Psalm 31:13–15, 19)

When David had nothing, he still had everything—because he lived on the promises of God. He had heard God's whisper in the night, and he allowed that still, small voice to speak louder than his worries.

My mom had a lot in common with David. Whenever I was going through a difficult time as a boy or a young man, she would always tell me, "Ron, you need to make a decision. You

must decide to live on the promises."

I knew what she meant. The promises of God.

"But Mom," I would say to her, "promises won't pay the bills!"

Yet somehow, through all the lean years, the bills did get paid. We may not have had much in our house, but we had God's Word, and Mom clung to it every day. In the back of her Bible, on the extra white pages, she did what a lot of the old-timers used to do: She wrote out God's promises.

There were promises for healing, promises for provision, promises for when you were afraid, promises for when you needed direction. We even had one of those old "Promise Boxes," shaped like a little loaf of bread, on the kitchen table. It was stuffed with promises written on tattered and well-thumbed cards. That sort of thing is a little out of fashion these days, and some might say the promises were quoted out of context. But do you know what? My mom lived on them, and they sustained her.

Something else she did meant more to me than anything. She wrote out the names of all of us kids in the back of her Bible, and next to each name she wrote a promise from the Bible that was appropriate for each of us. For as long as I can remember, my life has been linked with a promise of God.

To base your life on the promises of God, to hear and bene-fit from God's whispers in the darkness, you must be con-vinced of several things. God tells us that we must believe that *He is* and that *He is the rewarder* of those who seek *Him* (Hebrews 11:6). His Word shows us again and again that faith and obedience are the keys that unlock His power and blessing in our lives.

At a little town called Ziklag on the Philistine frontier, David faced the loss of everything. Raiders had swept through his camp and taken everything. David and his little ragtag army had lost their wives, children, and all their provisions. The men were so grieved and angry that they talked about stoning him.

Very possibly, it was the worst moment of David's life to that point. The darkest of the dark. The lowest of the low.

And what did he do?

David strengthened himself in the LORD his God. (1 Samuel 30:6)

How did he do that? Scripture says that he "inquired of the LORD" (v. 8). He turned to the Word of God. David had learned times beyond counting that when you lose everything you have, you seek God and His Word. You rebuild your life on His promises.

"DON'T GIVE UP!"

Recently, I was fascinated to hear about a unique form of Chinese puppet theater. Mr. Yong Fong, a fifth-generation puppetry expert, explained that traditional Chinese hand-puppet theater is acted out on two levels at the same time.

The lower level shows the characters as they progress moment by moment through the trials and tribulations of the play. On the upper level, however, the audience can see how the play *concludes*, as the villains are punished and the heroes are rewarded.

Because the audience can already see the outcome by looking up, they're not overly worried when the situation looks grave and the bad guys start to gain the upper hand. Instead, they get vocally involved. They begin shouting encouragement at the harried characters on the lower level. "Don't quit!" they shout. "Don't stop! Don't give up! We *know* you're going to make it!"

That's the privilege God gives to His children. That's the message He would like to whisper in our ears in those nights when worry keeps us awake. No matter what our present circumstances, no matter how gloomy the day or how heavy our heart, God's Word tells us that His children will overcome. He

will provide. He will comfort. He will heal. He will deliver. If not now, then later. If not in this life, then in the next.

Hebrews 12 tells us that, even when we feel like we're alone, we are surrounded by a great cloud of witnesses encouraging us to believe and press on. If you listen closely, you might hear David's voice urging you to grasp the promises of God.

You *might* hear David. But then again, on that subject, my mom might drown him out.

CHAPTER SIX

"Trust Me"

*B*ack in the seventies, a popular phrase made the rounds in Christian circles. You'd see it on buttons and bumper stickers and lapel pins.

"TRY JESUS."

For some reason, it always hit me as just a bit flat. Or trite. It sounded a little too much like "Try Dipsi-Cola" or "Try Chet's Frozen Dinners."

I will admit, however, that there are biblical grounds for a phrase like that. After all, in Psalm 34 David says, "Oh, taste and see that the LORD is good." God does seem to be encouraging people to "try Him out"—to wade in the waters of His goodness and grace and find out firsthand that He is everything He says He is.

But as soothing as wading in the shallows might be, real comfort and healing don't occur until we get in over our heads and strike out for the deep. Real trust doesn't occur until we've committed *the full weight* of our hopes, dreams, and expectations—our very lives—into His hands.

"Trying Jesus" sounds too much like the fear of commitment that is so common in today's culture. Young men and women speak of "trying marriage." You know: If it works and it feels good, fine. But if it gets too hard or too painful or too dull

or too confining…well, it's time to move on and "try" something else.

An Insight at the Altar

I remember our wedding day so well. Joyce and I graduated from college together on Friday night and were married on Saturday. This boy was so in love that he didn't know if he was coming or going. What a fun courtship we'd had! We'd served on traveling ministry teams together and had gone to basketball games together. (She was a cheerleader, and I was a basketball player.) I didn't care much what we did as long as I could be with her.

But then something happened. I suddenly found myself standing at an altar before a pastor with a Bible in his hands, reading us our vows. He said things like "forsaking all others" and "in sickness and in health" and "till death do you part."

That's when it struck me.

"Gosh," I thought, "He's talking about *forever.*"

This was serious business, and I knew without a doubt that God Himself was watching and listening. This wasn't just hanging out with my girlfriend and drinking Cokes and playing Putt-Putt golf. The pastor was asking me to *make a commitment.* In fact, he was looking right at me and saying, "as long as you both shall live." That's a long time! A lifetime. I was making a commitment to Joyce that would remain in effect as long as there was blood in our veins and breath in our bodies. This wasn't a trial run or a "let's see how this works." We were burning all our bridges behind us. We were joining our very lives together before God, and there was no going back.

Sometimes I have engaged couples tell me that they'd like to write their own vows for their wedding. "Fine," I say, "but you need to have someone else marry you, because I won't." Maybe I'm getting bolder with age, but I draw a firm line on this. I've discovered that many of the "vows" being written today are syrupy, weak, and basically noncommittal. Instead of

saying "till death do us part," they say things like "as long as we both shall love."

Now what does *that* mean? How long is that? Until the first fight? The first illness? The first dirty diaper? Until the first five-pound gain? Until the first wrinkle or the first gray hair? That's a line for someone who would be better off going to Hertz Rent-a-Ring instead of purchasing a wedding band.

The kind of trust David speaks about in Psalm 37 has commitment running straight through it—like the copper in an electric cord. One commentator describes it as a "submission to His will in the hope of His resolution of the dilemma. It speaks of an active obedience and reliance upon the Lord."

Try Jesus, yes. But to truly *trust* Him means putting yourself completely into His hands.

Psalm 37 is a beautiful picture of putting your trust in the Lord when all the circumstances of life are screaming that you should do something else. David looked around him, and at first glance it appeared that those who weren't trusting in the Lord were doing much better than those who were. It seemed like those who planned evil schemes and cooked up dishonest scams were not only getting away with it—but prospering! The arrogant godless seemed to be growing in power, influence, confidence, and wealth, while the righteous in the land were just scraping along, barely making it (vv. 7, 12, 14, 16, 35).

But David had made up his mind. He was God's man, heart and soul. He was going to place his full weight on the Lord's faithfulness—come what may. That's trust. That's not only the kind of trust that brings salvation, it's also the kind that brings comfort and healing in the dark times.

Whenever I think about trust, I'm reminded of the time I backed over the edge of a cliff.

OVER THE EDGE

Some of the macho, outdoorsy guys from our church thought it would be entertaining to have me go rappelling with them. It

was one of those times when I was reluctant to refuse because I was afraid I might offend somebody.

I should have refused anyway.

I remember climbing for hours to get to the top of the cliff and then standing around for additional hours waiting for them to prepare harnesses, check equipment, and tie off ropes. While they were getting ready, I ventured gingerly over to the edge of the cliff to take a peek. I could see the ground (through passing clouds), but since we were on an overhang, I couldn't see the face of the cliff at all. That's about the time I began to perspire.

Gentleman that I am, I let all the other guys go first. (Maybe a major storm would roll in, and we could all go home early!) But the inevitable moment came when there was nobody left on the cliff but me…and the guy holding the rope.

He motioned to me with a smile. It was my turn.

He cinched me in, and I gripped the rope like there was no tomorrow. You know, walking over the edge of a cliff wouldn't be one of my favorite activities under almost any circumstance. But the most hideous thing about rappelling is that you have to walk over the edge of the cliff *backwards*. You can't see where you're going, and the moment comes when you have to step off terra firma into empty space.

That, my friends, is commitment.

I remember thinking, *Lord, if I fall, at least let me land on the guy who thought up this idea.*

As I looked one last time at the rope, at the special knot, and at the thick tree to which I was tied, I realized something significant. For the second time in my life, I was totally putting my life in the hands of another human being. Joyce was the first. And now there was this grinning bald guy in a flannel shirt on the other end of my rope.

I stepped off the edge.

That's the kind of trust David is talking about in this psalm. It's no weak "try Jesus" kind of dibble dabbling in the faith. It

means trusting the weight of your life to the rope of God's faithfulness, with no possibility of turning back. It's presenting your life to Christ as a living sacrifice—and refusing to crawl off the altar.

OUT OF CONTROL?

You aren't truly trusting until you're slightly out of control—like Peter when he stepped out on the water. You aren't truly trusting until you've leaned so hard on Him that if you fell, you couldn't catch yourself. Trust means setting aside all secondary options, backup systems, and emergency parachutes. Trust says, "I've gone so far now that there's no return for me. If God doesn't save me and hold me up, I'll go under."

Over twenty-five years ago, we began our ministry in Beaverton with a small congregation. To be honest, I could have taken the whole church and a couple of visitors out for pie in a Dodge van. On a good Sunday, we had a dozen people rattling around in a building that would seat a hundred and forty.

My problem right then, however, wasn't the smallness of the congregation. It was that I felt terribly inadequate to pastor. I didn't feel capable of shepherding even a dozen sheep.

I remember our first service, when I preached to those twelve people. It was a unique experience. One of the men who came through the door was dressed like an old trapper who had just come down from the mountains after a long winter. Another man hummed. Not once or twice, but through the whole service. Really, it didn't matter much to me whether they *all* wore coonskin caps and hummed "Dixie." We needed all the people who were there and were plenty glad to have them.

Still, I felt so insufficient for the task. The moment the service was over, I wanted to be alone. I walked into one of the side rooms, got down on my knees, and pressed my face against the cool metal of a folding chair. I was so troubled and burdened. I began to pray and cry out to the Lord.

"Lord," I said, "I'm in over my head and You know it. What can I possibly give these people or say to them that will help them or change their lives? You know I'm not a very good preacher. You know I'm not Mr. Charisma or Mr. Personality. Lord, what am I going to do? What are *You* going to do?

Joyce and I had been married for only a couple of years. We'd been youth directors, and then, amazingly, we were offered a good-sized church of four to five hundred people.

We were also offered Beaverton—with twelve people.

I thought, *Boy, if we take the big church, we're going to look wonderful. If we just maintain that church for four or five years, people will say, "Boy, he's an awesome guy. He's got a big church."*

But what if God called us to Beaverton? (I had a strange feeling that He might.)

I sat down with my wife and said, "Joyce, let's talk. I want to know something here. I want to make sure you understand that if we take this church of five hundred, people are going to think we're awesome. If we just hold onto what we have and don't drive anybody away, people will say, 'Aren't they great?' But if we take a church of a dozen people and maintain a dozen people, they'll say, 'That Ron Mehl is a loser.'"

Joyce shook her head firmly. "Nobody would say that, Ron."

"Well, maybe not. But here's my real concern, Joycie. If we go to this little church, I don't want you looking around after a couple of years and thinking, *Why did I marry this loser? I could have married someone else—even a REAL preacher.* So let's make this decision together. If God calls us to Beaverton, it's possible we could end up ministering to twelve people the rest of our lives. If the Lord asks us to do that, are you willing? Because if you are, then I am."

I've learned since, of course, that you should never underestimate the faith and courage of Joyce Mehl. She was ready to take Beaverton in a heartbeat—or anywhere else in the world—if that's where the Lord was leading.

So…we took a deep breath and backed over the edge of the cliff. Together. We put our trust in the Lord to meet our needs and prosper the ministry as it pleased Him.

As the days went by, the Lord began to speak to me about our little flock. I thought I heard Him telling me that He was committed to doing a great work in Beaverton, but it was really hard for me to believe because I certainly didn't believe in *me*.

Then one Saturday morning I had an encounter with the Lord that changed everything.

A MOMENT IN HIS SANCTUARY

I arrived at our little church building while the robins were still announcing the new day and the grass was wet with dew. I fumbled with the keys for a minute in the morning chill, then let myself in. The truth was that I'd been a bit discouraged that week about the church's prospects. I'd been thinking, *Lord, nothing's going to happen here. These are the greatest, dearest people in the world, but we're still only a handful.*

I went into my office but couldn't settle down. Restless, I walked back into the cool dimness of the sanctuary. The morning sunlight, red gold and mellow, poured in through the windows.

Suddenly I found myself on my knees, weeping my eyes out.

It's difficult to explain—and I'm not sure I should even try. But in that moment, I felt the immediate presence of God as never before in my life. Suddenly, He was just *there*, and it almost took my breath away. I didn't just fall to my knees, I was *pushed* to my knees.

In that moment, the Lord spoke to me about doing a great work in Beaverton. No, it wasn't in an audible voice, but I knew very well what He was saying. And I also knew that He was going to do a work in Beaverton *whether I was there or not.* He could do it with me or without me. So He was offering me a choice. If I stayed and put the weight of my trust in Him, He

would use me. If I left, He would use someone else—and if He could use *me,* He could use anybody!

It was an encounter I went back to again and again over the following months and years. No matter how I struggled in my ministry, no matter how many empty chairs I saw on a Sunday morning, I could go back to the time when I felt the overwhelming presence of God—when He spoke to me, and I wept before Him and put my trust in Him to work through me.

In Proverbs 3:5–6, David's wise son Solomon wrote:

> Trust in the LORD with all your heart,
> And lean not on your own understanding;
> In all your ways acknowledge Him,
> And He shall direct your paths.

There are conditional and unconditional promises in the Bible. This one is conditional. It is dependent upon our obedience. In other words, until you make a decision to trust Him with all your heart—until you lean your full weight upon Him—He's *not* going to direct your paths, He's *not* going to make a way, and He's *not* going to work things out.

Trusting in God isn't a risk. Listen, God actually knows in advance who will be the next Miss America and who will win the NCAA basketball championship. I can trust in God because He knows me and has a plan that will get me from where I am to where I need to be. Wasn't that what Paul was saying in Romans 8:28? "And we know that all things work together for good to those who love God, to those who are the called according to His purpose." Paul says, "I'm confident because I know God makes no mistakes."

Are you confident and convinced of God's work? Is God working too slowly for you? Does His plan seem too hard? Paul says, "I can trust God because there is purpose behind everything He does and allows."

Peter came to such a moment in his life, too. At a cross-

roads moment in Jesus' ministry, there were many who walked away from Him—and just a few who vowed to trust Him no matter what.

> From that time many of His disciples went back and walked with Him no more. Then Jesus said to the twelve, "Do you also want to go away?" Then Simon Peter answered Him, "Lord, to whom shall we go? You have the words of eternal life. Also we have come to believe and know that You are the Christ, the Son of the living God." (John 6:66–69)

I love that. Peter had already backed over the cliff. Peter had already driven his climber's piton deep into the Rock, and his whole weight was hanging on the strength of it.

"Lord," he was saying, "You speak of going away, but where else would I go? What else am I going to do? You've got everything I have. I've given up my business, my old relationships, my old pleasures, my bank account, my very life. I've staked everything on You—all my hopes, all my dreams, everything I am and have. It's too late to look for any other options, even if I wanted to."

That's trust.

Yes, at that point Peter's words were stronger than his resolve, and he would stumble badly along the way. He would fail and falter and fall. But he would also come back—more determined than ever.

Of course he would. Once you've heard God's whisper in the dark, you hold onto Him as though He were life itself.

And He is.

CHAPTER SEVEN

"I Am with You"

The orphans cried themselves to sleep every night, and the volunteers at the orphanage were at their wits' end.

Many of the children had been rescued right off the streets. Now, instead of eating out of trash cans and sleeping on doorsteps, they went to bed at night with full stomachs, laid their heads on soft pillows, and slept between crisp, clean sheets. For the first time in their lives, they had adults who really cared for them, protected them, and comforted them.

But still they cried.

Finally, someone had a flash of insight. The children were fearful and fretful at bedtime not because they were hungry, but because they were worried about tomorrow. Yes, they went to bed with full stomachs, but they had no confidence that there would be food in the morning. Nothing in their brief experience of life had given them any reason to expect consistency, stability, or security. True, they had tasted kindness and provision today—but tomorrow? It might all blow away! Tomorrow might find them on their own again—hungry, unloved, and alone.

So they wept.

When they realized why the children were crying, the

orphanage staff came up with a new procedure. Every night when they tucked the children into bed, they gave them each a large bread roll to hold or tuck under the pillow. The roll would be there in the night if they were hungry, and it would be there in the morning, a reassurance of the loving care and provision that was now theirs.

From that night on, there were no more sniffles and stifled sobs. The children went right to sleep.

Our friends Bob and Gayle Potter experienced something similar as foster parents. Some of the children they've cared for through the years have come to them from unspeakably abusive backgrounds. The stories of neglect and cruelty toward these little ones break your heart. Some are children of drug dealers and have known nothing in life but fear, hostility, and deprivation.

Little Sasha came to the Potters' home from such a background. She was a pale, thin, undersized six-year-old. Her wide brown eyes were filled with fear. When the authorities found her, she was cold, hungry, bruised, and unable to trust *anyone*—even people as loving and kind as Bob and Gayle.

One morning not long after Sasha had come to stay with them, Gayle noticed some coconut shreds on the counter. Now you and I might not have given those crumbs a second thought, but with the everything-in-its-place kitchen Gayle keeps, the bits of coconut immediately signaled something unusual. Gayle noticed a little more coconut on the floor, below the counter, and a little more in the middle of the kitchen floor.

Gayle realized that the coconut shreds formed a loose trail. *Like Hansel and Gretel's bread crumbs,* she thought. *I wonder where they lead.*

The trail wound its way out of the kitchen, down the hall, and into a bedroom—Sasha's bedroom. That was when Gayle discovered that Sasha had hidden food *everywhere* in her room—under the bed, under her mattress, in her dresser, in

her closet—all because she was afraid that, come morning, there wouldn't be any.

At dinner, Sasha would eat like a sumo wrestler. But still, night after night, she would smuggle food into her room—food that wasn't particularly fresh by the time Gayle tracked it down!

Children of God never have to go to bed at night wondering whether or not He will be there when they wake up. They never have to wonder about His provision. "Dwell in the land," David wrote, "and feed on His faithfulness" (Psalm 37:3). Or, as the NIV renders it, "Dwell in the land and enjoy safe pasture."

It's one of the main things God wants to whisper to you in the night.

GRAZING 101

By the time he wrote Psalm 37, David had seen a lot of life. He had already been a fugitive, a warrior, and a king. In his heart, however, he was still a shepherd.

Asaph, another psalmist, wrote this about David:

He also chose David His servant,
And took him from the sheepfolds;
From following the ewes that had young He brought him,
To shepherd Jacob His people....
So he shepherded them according to the integrity of his heart,
And guided them by the skillfulness of his hands.
(Psalm 78:70–72)

David had graduated from God's school of leadership—Sheep-Pen State. He remembered what it was like to lead a flock through the wilderness and how vulnerable and dependent those sheep were. He remembered the pleasure and satisfaction he felt when he led his flock to a place of safety and abundance...in green pastures...beside still waters.

David knew how to lead people because of his experience with a bunch of woolly animals! And so in Psalm 37:3, this shepherd-king tells us to place our trust in a greater Shepherd-King: "Trust in the LORD, and do good; dwell in the land, and feed on His faithfulness."

That word *feed* is the same one used to describe how a domestic animal eats. Have you ever watched sheep? It doesn't exactly set your pulse racing. After all, what do they do all day? Eat and rest. Rest and eat. Eat and eat and rest and rest. It's not as though they grab a quick breakfast and run off to do a thousand other things. They pretty much eat all morning. And *then* what do they do? Run errands? Go into town? Patrol the fence lines? Plant more grass seed? No. They graze some more.

Grazing takes time. They stay at it, trusting the shepherd to protect them from predators and lead them along to fresh pasture when they need to move…and not before.

This is the Lord's message to us: "Just stay near Me—as close as you can. Don't run yourself ragged looking for help and hope. Don't keep consulting this person, that person, and the other person. Talk to Me every time you think of it. Read portions of My Word and then chew and chew and chew on them. Stay in My truth. Crowd your way into My presence. Drink from My stream. Stay, stay, stay. And rest in My faithful love and care." Instead of allowing ourselves to be troubled, worried, or led astray by our circumstances, David urges us to feed, like a humble sheep, on the faithfulness of God—to graze safely in God's good pasture.

FEED ON HIS FAITHFULNESS

How do you do that? How do you feed on God's faithfulness? What does that really mean?

When we speak of the faithfulness of God, we're talking about the firmness, security, and stability of His character—of all that He is. In other psalms, David describes God as his "Rock," his "Refuge," and his "Fortress." In the New Testament,

James speaks of a God in whom "there is no variation or shadow of turning" (James 1:17), which means that there are never any eclipses with God. There's never anything that stands between Him and me. There's never a time when the sun of His love and His healing are going to be blocked from me. No matter what I see going on around me, nothing will stop Him from delivering to me what He has purposed to give.

We can depend on such a God. We can find in such a God the rest, comfort, and peace for which our hearts long.

These are some of the words that God longs to whisper in our ears in those turbulent, anxious nights of our lives. "I am with you. You can count on Me."

Pasture in His stability, David, the old shepherd, tells us. Graze on His security and truth. The world around you may change. The fortunes of some will soar, while others will suffer loss. There will be ups and downs, highs and lows, sunlight and storms, wide spaces and tight places. There will be temptations to become frantic, running here and there, trying this and that. But you, child of God, just be at peace and rest secure. Feed on God's provision and rest in His faithful love and protection.

Enjoy safe pasture.

If He has provided for your needs yesterday and today, He will provide for you tomorrow. If He saved you yesterday, he will keep you today...and tomorrow and tomorrow and tomorrow.

While the Israelites were wandering in the wilderness, God's manna was there for them to collect every morning. They were not allowed to take more than they needed or to hoard it or store it. If they tried, it became rancid and wormy. Inedible. So every morning God repeated the miracle. They received their "daily bread" for that day only. But it was always there.

The medicine for those dark times in our lives isn't like a pill you swallow for an instant cure. It's more like insulin for a diabetic. It's something that will keep you alive and well for the rest

of your life, but you need to have it and partake of it *every day.*

God is faithful, no matter what the situation. When you go to bed at night—even if you have nothing in your hands or under your pillow—even if there are no visible signs of success and blessing in your life—you can trust Him to provide in the morning.

I'm reminded that when Jesus invited us to "ask," "seek," and "knock," He literally said, "keep on asking," "keep on seeking," "keep on knocking." Don't do it just once and then try something else. When it comes to a relationship with the living God, we must ask, seek, and knock continually.

And what does the Good Shepherd promise to us if we do?

"For everyone who asks receives, and he who seeks find, and to him who knocks it will be opened." (Luke 11:10)

This isn't some temporary cure or fix. It's a life direction. For the rest of your life, if you keep asking, seeking, and knocking, you will continually receive, find, and have the doors opened. Or as David puts it, if you keep grazing in His pastures, "verily thou shalt be fed" (Psalm 37:3, KJV).

Throughout the forty verses of Psalm 37, David is leading us to reorient our whole lives toward God—showing us how to trust in the Lord and rest in Him *in the face of external circumstances that scream the exact opposite at us.* He is teaching us to delight in the Lord, even when we cannot delight in everything going on around us. He's teaching us to trust the Lord and not to fret. And He's teaching us to feed on the Lord every day of our lives.

It's what God would whisper to us every night of our lives—if we would only listen.

SOMEONE WITH ME

I remember a period of time as a boy when I was growing extremely fast. I was eating poor Mom out of house and home

and growing out of all my clothes at a pace that must have alarmed her. Of course every boy loves that, and it was fun to dream of becoming a pro basketball player.

But the rapid growth had its downsides, too, and it wasn't just wearing "high water" jeans to school. Sometimes in the middle of the night, my shins and legs would begin aching so badly that I could hardly stand it. Now, of course, I understand that it was no big deal—just common growing pains. But back then I didn't know what was happening to me, and I was worried as well as hurting. It would get so bad that I would weep with the pain. Unable to sleep, I would go downstairs and lie on the couch.

Mom would come out of her room in her bathrobe and sit beside me on the couch in the dark. She would rub my legs and shins real hard, and after a while, I felt better. Even though the pain didn't completely go away, it was great to have her there. It meant a lot to know that she was with me in my pain and that she cared so much. And the next night, when the pains came back, she would do it again.

She was faithful. She was always there. Not only for the physical pains, but for all the other pains a bashful boy experiences as he becomes an adolescent and tries to make his way in a hostile world. Mom was with me through those times, and I depended on her.

In chapter 4, I talked about our friends Chuck and Lorna. When their little boy was killed, they could find no relief for their terrible pain, for the hurt and grief. Only by turning to the Lord did they find help. Did the pain go away? No. But they allowed that crushing hurt to drive them into the Lord's arms every day. Every day they took their pain to Him. Every day they fed on His truth and drank from His healing stream. Every day they let Him dry their tears.

Yes, the nights were very, very difficult.

Because of the terrible memories and images in her mind, Lorna was so frightened to go to bed that she not only read the

Bible before she went to bed, *but she tucked it under her pillow and slept on it.* Like the orphans who took the bread to bed with them and slept with it under their pillows, this grieving young mother pillowed her head on God's faithful Word. How she depended on those whispered reassurances from her Lord and Shepherd! And when she woke up in the morning, there it was. Another day's comfort. Another day's strength. Another day's provision.

Yes, there are still moments when the pain comes surging back. When they see a little boy who looks like their Landon looked, when they think about how old he would be now if he had lived, when something for some reason reminds them, the memories come, piercing so deep.

What do they do? They go back to the Lord. They stay in His pasture. They feed on His faithfulness. Yes, there are some hurts that God can cure in an instant. There are some things God can fix right now. But other hurts linger. The death of a child, a prodigal son or daughter, the loss of a mate, a broken marriage, an injury or disease, financial failure—or any one of life's deep disappointments. These are hurts and troubles that require His touch every day—and every night.

NIGHT BY NIGHT, MORNING BY MORNING

I have only to remember a Sunday morning some years ago when Amy, sitting at the grand piano near the platform at our church, sang "Great Is Thy Faithfulness." I sat there wiping away the tears, thinking, *How can she sing that? It doesn't seem as though God has been faithful to her at all!* It had only been a few months since her husband of eleven years had deserted her and run away with another woman. What rejection! What shame and hurt!

Through it all, Amy has learned to feed on God's safe pasture. That's why she can lift her voice and sing:

Great is Thy faithfulness, O God my Father,
There is no shadow of turning with Thee.
Thou changest not, Thy compassions they fail not,
As Thou has been, Thou forever wilt be.
Great is Thy faithfulness, great is Thy faithfulness,
Morning by morning new mercies I see!
All I have needed Thy hand hath provided,
Great is Thy faithfulness, Lord unto me![1]

Amy, like David, could sing *in spite* of her circumstances. She had tasted of His faithfulness. She was resting in green pastures, beside still waters, where no predator could harm her.

The Good Shepherd Himself has seen to that.

1. Thomas O. Chisholm, "Great Is Thy Faithfulness," © 1923. *Renewal 1951* by Hope Publishing Co., Carol Streat, IL 60188. All rights reserved. Used by permission.

CHAPTER EIGHT

"Step into
My Strength"

*D*elight yourself also in the LORD," David coun-
seled, "and He shall give you the desires of your
heart" (Psalm 37:4).

That's an easy assignment when everything happens to be
going your way!

I can remember a few golden, exceedingly rare days on the
golf course when I just seemed to have "the touch." I couldn't
do anything wrong. The wind was at my back, my muscles
were loose, my timing was right, my eye was clear, my stroke
was strong, my putts were unerring, and I could seemingly
drop that little white ball wherever I wanted it to go.

Talk about delightful!

It's especially fun when you're golfing with your buddies,
and you get to pretend like shooting a 72 is the most normal
and natural thing in the world.

As your friends shake their heads in bewilderment, you say,
"Why *of course* my opening drive went 325 yards and landed
on the green. *Naturally* I sank my twenty-foot putt. Did you
really expect anything less?"

You feel so good about life that you become a big spender
and offer to buy everyone Cokes at the clubhouse.

But then there are those *other* times.

Times when you feel as if you couldn't get the pesky ball into the cup if you were on the Bonneville Salt Flats and the hole was as large as a bomb crater. You can't do anything right. The wind is against you, your muscles are tight, your timing is wrong, your vision seems hazy, your stroke is feeble, and your putts have depraved minds of their own.

Those are days when you certainly don't want to buy the Cokes at the clubhouse. You don't even want to see the clubhouse. You feel like stomping off the course and saying, "This is supposed to be fun? Why do I do this? I'm *never* coming back!" The word *delight* just doesn't describe what you're feeling!

When he wrote Psalm 37, David had been looking at the circumstances around him, and *delight* wasn't exactly written across the sky for him, either. Careless, wanton, power-hungry people were swinging across the land like a wrecking ball. Good, decent people were being trampled. Greedy, unprincipled men and women were clawing their way into positions of power and influence—and it all looked so ridiculously easy for them. David's heart was troubled. Worry dogged him day and night like a toothache.

These are precisely the times David was talking about when he said, "Delight yourself in the LORD."

STEP AWAY FROM YOUR STRENGTH

In the language of the Bible, *delight* is a soft word. A feminine word. A word that implies responding to and luxuriating in the attentions of another. It is the picture of a new bride who has deliberately chosen to seek her happiness and fulfillment in her husband. She yields to him and finds delight.

Here's another way to understand it: *To delight means to step away from your own strength and find strength in another.*

When I was a boy, my buddy Raymond and I could strut around and act as cocky and confident as any other little boys our age. We were twice as brave (and probably twice as mouthy) when we were together than when we were by our-

selves. Sometimes that got us into trouble with the older, bigger boys. They saw through all our bluster and demanded that we walk our talk.

On occasion, a couple of them were more than ready to put us in our places. These were usually guys from another neighborhood—guys who didn't know about our secret weapon.

Dave.

Dave was Raymond's very strong, very athletic big brother. And Dave wasn't just any big brother. He had a strong protective streak in him and didn't take his brotherly duties casually. He took it personally when he caught anyone giving grief to his little brother—or his little brother's friend!

Dave would heed our call and step into our situation, casting a long shadow. In those moments, Raymond and I were more than content to let our tough guy image go by the board. We were delighted to stand behind Dave and watch him wreak havoc on our enemies. We loved the fire in his eyes. We were thrilled beyond measure to see him stab the air with his forefinger and hear him say, "If you EVER mess with these kids again I'm going to FIND you and make sure that you are VERY, VERY sorry."

The only trouble with that arrangement was that Dave wasn't omnipresent. He couldn't always be where we were. He wasn't always within hailing distance in an emergency, and in those days we didn't have beepers or cell phones.

But King David knew that we can *always* delight in the Lord. We can always count on His presence and strength. He is always within range of our faintest cry for help in the night. And He loves to have us step out of our own puny strength and into His mighty shadow. He loves to have us find our delight and fulfillment and security in Him.

King David was as tough and courageous as they come (remember Goliath?). But he had no problem at all stepping back from his own strength and taking refuge in the Lord. In the Twenty-first Psalm, he wrote:

O LORD, the king rejoices in your strength.
How great is his joy in the victories you give!
You have granted him the desire of his heart.
(Psalm 21:1–2, NIV)

That's the very same thought he expresses in Psalm 37:4:

Delight yourself also in the LORD,
And He shall give you the desires of your heart.

Delight means *to not be strong for yourself.* In other words, let God do this. And as you do, He will give to you those very things for which your heart longs. Pour your energies into delighting in Him, and let Him work things out.

Can you hear His whisper? "My son, My daughter, you don't have to make everything right. You don't have to work everything out. You're trying so hard to be a little god on your own. Would you—just for a while—put all of that aside? Would you step back from your worrying and scheming and trying to manipulate events...and just delight in Me?"

That certainly sounds good. But it might not be as easy for some people as it is for others. Some people are real doers. They're action-oriented, Martha types who like to jump into a situation, rattle around, and make things happen. It is neither easy nor comfortable for them to yield control to another— even to God.

YOU CAN ONLY DO WHAT YOU CAN DO

My best friend, Roy Hicks Jr., was a very godly man, but he was also a "doer." Right up until his recent, untimely death, he was bright, competent, and energetic; he liked to roll up his sleeves and get things done. It seemed to me he could do just about anything he set his mind to. I always felt that he could wade into a blackwater swamp and organize the alligators into a hospitality committee.

So when Roy, who loved me very much, heard that I had been diagnosed with leukemia, he naturally wanted to *do* something about it.

He used to call me every morning, and after he heard the news, he kept saying, "Ron, I'm just sick about this. I'm so burdened. What can I do? Is there anything I can do? Is there any way I can help?"

What a great friend! It really frustrated him that he couldn't throw his gifts and energies and love into some sort of plan to help me out.

One evening he wanted to be alone and do some praying. He got into his Jeep with his little dog, Jericho, and drove out an old logging road into the woods, west of his home in Eugene, Oregon. He parked the Jeep on a wide spot in the road and opened the door to get out. As he did, two things happened in quick succession. First, Jericho jumped out and ran straight into the woods, barking his little head off. Then, as Roy got out of the Jeep, he dropped his glasses on the road and stepped on them.

Great, he thought. *Just great.*

He walked into the shadowed forest, praying, "Lord, what can I do? There have to be some things I can do for my friend."

He stayed out in the woods a couple of hours, praying for me—but feeling no reassurance at all. Then it began to grow dark. It was time to leave. Roy called for the dog.

"Jericho! Jericho!"

But Jericho didn't come. There was no snuffling in the bushes, no barks, nothing. The woods were silent in the gathering darkness.

Oh boy, he thought. *Now I am in trouble. Jeff and Kay are going to be beside themselves.* He knew how much his wife and young son loved the little rascal.

"JERICHO! JERICHO!"

He called and called, but there was no response. If anything, the silence seemed to deepen.

Well, this is it. This is too much. I might as well go home. My best friend has leukemia, I broke my glasses, and I lost the family dog. All in all, it's been quite an evening.

He climbed back into his Jeep and drove home, feeling as miserable as could be.

When he woke up early the next morning, he thought, *I'm going back.* He drove back to the woods and began hollering again for Jericho. But there was no Jericho.

Finally, Roy gave up. What else could he do? He'd done everything he knew to do, but he couldn't find the dog. His friend had a life-threatening disease, but there was nothing he could do about that either.

He cranked up the Jeep and yelled one last time out the open door. "Jericho! HEEERRRE JERR-I-CHO!" Just as he began to slam the door, he heard a familiar yelp and a scurry of little legs. Jericho came bounding through the trees out into the clearing, ran to the Jeep, and jumped up into Roy's lap.

Roy told me later how the Lord spoke so clearly to his heart in that moment. "See...don't worry. I found your dog, I can heal your friend...and you can buy your own glasses."

From that moment on, Roy told me, he felt released from his terrible worry about my health. He could do what he could do, and what he couldn't do, he would leave with the Lord. My dear friend placed me back in God's hands—where I had actually been all along.

It's just a simple story, but I think it makes an important point. There is a lot we need to do about our situations, a lot we *should* do, and a few things we may or may not do. But there are times in life when we just need to step back and say, "Lord, this is too serious, too hard, and too heavy, and there's nothing else I can do. I'm going to direct my energies and emotions into delighting in You and let You work on my behalf."

God really loves it when we do that.

There comes a point when you don't know which way to go in the woods, you don't know which way to run, and you don't

know which way to look. There are times when changing a situation is simply beyond your power. You really can't do anything about your friend's leukemia. You can't find anything that's been lost, heal everything that's been wounded, and fix everything that's been broken. But you can step into the strength of the Lord God whose "arm...is not too short to save, nor his ear too dull to hear" (Isaiah 59:1, NIV).

THE GIFT OF DEPENDENCE

God loves us so much that every once in a while, He arranges circumstances that are simply too big for us to handle and too heavy for us to carry. His desire is not that these things crush us, but that through them we learn to find our help and delight in Him.

God loves to arrange the odds in our life, so that when the victory does come, we'll know who really deserves the credit. Look most anywhere in the pages of your Bible and you will see God arranging the odds—stacking the deck—and allowing His children to find themselves up against overwhelming circumstances. And then you hear Him saying things like, "Be still, and know that I am God," or "Stand still and see the salvation of the Lord."

God is a giving God. He wants to give us the desire of our hearts. But there are some things you'll never experience until you are ready to receive them by His hand. You can't work for these things. You can't obtain them by being sincere, doing good deeds, working your fingers to the bone, or trying very, very hard. God wants to *give* them to you. And that requires an attitude of humble dependence upon Him.

I see so many men and women who become impatient and insist on taking matters into their own hands. God doesn't seem to be leading them to a life partner, so they lower their standards and determine to go anywhere and do anything to find someone. God isn't prospering their business, so they compromise their convictions and cut ethical corners to make

it happen. God isn't blessing their ministry, so they pull a bunch of gimmicks and worldly tricks out of the bag to generate "success."

Some of these determined people actually achieve their goals. Yet what a price they pay! So often they ruin their lives in the process. They gain what they thought they wanted so badly, but there is no *delight*. There is only emptiness and regret.

I remember when we were building our new worship center, and a little bird flew in the open window. Of course it immediately panicked, caught in this foreign place. Several of us tried to help the poor, frantic thing. It flew into the walls. It flew into the glass doors. It circled around and around, exhausting itself and beating itself silly.

I wanted so much to help that little bird! How easy it would have been if it could just have trusted me! All I wanted to do was help it reach its goal. I knew where the bird wanted to be, and I had the power to get it there. All the bird needed to do was to sit still for a moment. It could have perched on my finger, and I would have gently taken it outside and let it go.

But it wouldn't let me.

It seemed determined to beat itself to pieces.

It's the same with you and me. What a terrible price we pay when we refuse the help of God and refuse to find our delight in Him. How He longs to help us and teach us and comfort us—if we would only be still before Him and wait on Him!

A Promise in the Night

Near the end of His earthly ministry, Jesus looked across the city of Jerusalem and His heart broke. He saw what was coming for the city. He knew the terrors and sorrows and desolation in store for her. But the people would not turn to Him! They refused to delight in the Lord. Jesus just shook His head and wept.

"O Jerusalem, Jerusalem, the one who kills the prophets and stones those who are sent to her! How often I wanted to gather your children together, as a hen gathers her chicks under her wings, but you were not willing! See! Your house is left to you desolate." (Matthew 23:37–38)

And our houses are desolate, too, when we refuse to delight in Him.

Do you crawl into bed at night with a weary, anxious heart? Is it possible you're trying too hard to make things happen? Is it possible you haven't stepped back from your own strengths and your own solutions? Could He be whispering gently to you even now—calling you to find your fulfillment and pleasure in Him?

Through Psalm 37, the Lord says to us what He said to David: "Those who reject Me may seem to prosper for a time. But that time is short! You know their end. They're not going to be satisfied with their gains. Their arms are going to break under the pressure of what they carry. You'll see them come, and you'll see them go. You'll see them rise, and you'll see them fall. But you, My child, step back, step back from your own strength and delight in Me. And if you do, I will give you the desires of your heart."

Can you hear His voice whispering that promise? It's one that can survive a bad golf day, a bad hair day, or those long, long hours before dawn.

Don't let your hopes grow dim.

Dare to delight in Him.

CHAPTER NINE

"Let Me Guide You"

Commit your way to the LORD;
trust in him and he will do this:
He will make your righteousness shine like the dawn,
the justice of your cause like the noonday sun.

PSALM 37:5–6, NIV

*I*t is a hard task to take your life in your own hands. It's a difficult burden to become, as the proud poet said, "the master of my fate" and "the captain of my soul." It is a frustrating, heartbreaking job to be your own travel agent through the short span of life granted us here on earth. Worrying and fretting over all of those details tend to take the joy out of the journey.

MAKING THE ARRANGEMENTS

Almost every two years, Joyce and I lead a group of excited fellow travelers to Israel. It's one of the greatest privileges and thrills we have in the ministry. For many of the people who go with us, it's the trip of a lifetime. They've dreamed about it for years. They've scrimped and saved and sacrificed to be able to go. They've waited much of their lives for an opportunity to

visit the Holy Land and to "walk where Jesus walked."

You wouldn't believe the excitement and anticipation as our El Al flight from New York City touches down in Tel Aviv and our group sets foot on Israeli soil. The spiritual heritage of this land is so rich for believers that it's impossible to leave Israel without feeling that you've left your own home. After all, it's *His* land, and that makes it ours, too.

A huge factor in the success of these trips is our relationship with an excellent, tried-and-true tour agency. Its experienced staffers do a great deal of careful planning and arranging all year long, before anyone has even signed up for the journey. They work hard to obtain the best fares, the best connections, and the best arrival and departure times. They double-check to make sure we have good ground transportation waiting for our arrival, nice hotels to stay in, friendly, knowledgeable guides to lead us, and good food to eat along the way.

Beyond all those provisions and connections, Joyce and I have worked with them to plan a variety of moving experiences and awe-inspiring places to see: Caesarea...Mt. Carmel...Megiddo, site of the future battle of Armageddon...a hike along the Jordan River...a sunrise over the Mount of Olives...a boat trip across the Sea of Galilee, where Jesus also walked...a solemn pilgrimage along "The Way of the Cross"...a precious hour of prayer and joyous worship at the Garden Tomb.

The tour company always does an excellent job for us because they've done this many times before and seem to know what people enjoy and appreciate most. They've been down those dusty Middle Eastern roads countless times. They've dealt with the airlines and the bus companies and the government officials. They know how to direct us to places that move us, intrigue us, and excite us.

On all our brochures, however, the tour company adds this significant line:

Special note: The tour guides reserve the right to alter the sequence of the daily itinerary and make substitutions in order to meet changes brought about by weather, airline delays, or as deemed necessary for the best interest and overall comfort of the group.

Do you know what? We trust them to do that. They have proven themselves trustworthy in a thousand different circumstances and situations. We count on them to take us here or take us there and to tell us to jump on this bus or wait for the next one. They have worked out the schedules and weighed the variables as much as possible, and if something goes wrong, we rely on them to know what to do, where to go, and whom to talk to. In short, *we commit our way to them.* We roll the responsibilities (and the anxieties) over onto their shoulders and look to them to do what's best. We're "along for the ride," and everyone has the time of their lives.

Imagine for a moment what it would be like if we stepped off the plane in Tel Aviv and said to those dear people on our tour, "Well, folks, we got you here, and now you're on your own. You have eleven days. There's a lot to see, so you'd better get to it. Meet back at the airport at such and such a time and we'll fly home. Shalom!"

Yes, a few of the more experienced travelers might possibly rise to the challenge, but most would be bewildered and deeply disappointed. They wouldn't know where to go. They wouldn't know what to do. They wouldn't know what tourist traps to avoid. They wouldn't know the best places to go or how to see what they want to see. They would get to the right places at the wrong times and the wrong places at the right times.

Besides that, there are certain areas and certain buildings that individuals simply cannot get into apart from an authorized tour. Following a tour guide allows you to see some

things and experience some things that individual tourists can't. And even if those individuals did manage to see a few significant things, the experience would be so time-consuming and stressful that there wouldn't be much opportunity for quietness, rest, meditation, worship, or companionship with new and old friends.

The bottom line, I guess, is that it wouldn't be much fun! Life is too short. A breath. A vapor. A fragile flower that opens at sunrise and wilts at night. I don't want to spend my brief life bogged down in details and worrying about arrangements I was never meant to handle. My way belongs to the Lord.

JOSHUA'S TOUR GUIDE

I can't help but think about the time in the Bible when Joshua was about to lead a tour group into the Holy Land. The difference was that he had about three and a half million men, women, and children to think about, and not a single person in that vast multitude—including Joshua—had ever set foot in the land before!

What a comfort it must have been to have the ark of the covenant of the Lord moving out ahead of the whole party. The ark signified the Lord's presence, not only among them, but also out ahead of them. And since it was the ark of the *covenant,* they were reminded that their tour guide was someone who kept all His promises.

Listen for a moment to the instructions the people received as they were about to cross the Jordan River and enter this strange, new land that would become their home:

> "When you see the ark of the covenant of the LORD your God, and the priests, the Levites, bearing it, then you shall set out from your place and go after it…that you may know the way by which you must go, for you have not passed this way before." (Joshua 3:3–4)

Joshua was reminding them, "You've never been this way before, and neither have I! But the Lord goes before us. Let's be careful to follow Him and place our trust for this journey in His hands. We've never been this way before, but He has!"

It's the same with our lives. We've never walked this journey called "life" before. When we open our eyelids in the morning, we face a day we've never lived before. When we celebrate a new year, we're standing at the threshold of 365 days that we know absolutely nothing about. We have no idea what a year, a month, or a day holds. We don't even know what's going to happen in the next sixty seconds. The phone might ring with news that would scramble all of our plans and literally change the course of our whole life. We don't know what awaits us around every corner.

But He knows!

He's the Lord of time and eternity. He's the Alpha and the Omega, the Beginning and the End.

David wrote, "Commit your way to the LORD; trust in him" (Psalm 37:5, NIV). The literal Hebrew rendering is "roll your way upon the LORD." It's the idea of getting rid of a heavy burden, of rolling it right off your shoulders. In other words:

- Give Him the itinerary of your life.
- Don't try to do it yourself.
- Don't try to be your own travel agent and tour guide.
- Don't try to make all your own connections and reservations.
- Don't spend your life chasing misplaced baggage.
- Don't carry the weight and worry of all the "maybes" and "what ifs" of life.

My friend, that's a prescription for a sleepless night! Roll it onto the Lord! Commit it to Him. If you've trusted Him for salvation and heaven, your ultimate destination, why not trust Him for everything else in between?

Paul had that very idea when he wrote: "He who did not spare His own Son, but delivered Him up for us all, how shall He not with Him also freely give us all things?" (Romans 8:32).

In other words, if Jesus made our reservations and paid for our ticket to heaven with His own blood, doesn't it make sense that He will take care of us along our journey? We can trust Him! Jesus has been through life before us. He's walked the path ahead of us. Scripture says He "was in all points tempted as we are, yet without sin" and that He is "the author and finisher of our faith" (Hebrews 4:15; 12:2). He has faced the temptations, experienced the longings, felt the pain, and even walked into death ahead of us so that He might remove its sting. And after He did that, He went home to prepare a place for us, getting it ready for our soon arrival (John 14:2–3).

He's done it all. He knows how to be Lord over a life.

So what happens if we experience frustrating delays in life? What happens if we encounter blocked roads or rained-out events or sudden changes in our plans or circumstances? We can trust Him! We can trust Him to lead us safely through this adventure called life—and then all the way home. When our flight touches down on the shining golden runway in Heaven's Interstellar Airport, and the light of eternal morning pours in through all the windows, we'll be able to say with the hymn writer, "Jesus led me all the way."

THE EMPTINESS OF "MY WAY"

To "commit your way to the Lord" is, of course, the very opposite of our world's man-centered philosophy. Frank Sinatra's trademark song, "I Did It My Way," sums it up well. When "Old Blue Eyes" belted out that number in front of audiences of adoring fans, everyone cheered.

It sounded good, I guess, when he sang it, but in my years of ministry, I've seen too many lives bruised, broken, and destroyed by that philosophy of life.

I've heard husbands and fathers say, "I did it my way!" as

they left a brokenhearted wife and bitter, grieving children in their wake.

I've heard young women say, "I did it my way!" and then spend the rest of their lives dealing with the consequences of an abortion or a child born out of wedlock.

I've heard teenagers say, "I did it my way!" as they made choices that crippled their potential, stole their joy, and limited their future service to the Lord.

Frankly, I don't want to do it "my way."

I know how weak and fallible I am. I know how short-sighted I can be and how prone I am to take the wrong direction or the wrong path. Life is too brief and too precious to waste in a futile effort to plan my own itinerary and chase my own baggage. I could have never made it to heaven going "my way"; I had to go *His* way because He is the Way, the Truth, and the Life. So if I'm trusting Him to get me to my final destination, why shouldn't I commit the *whole* journey to His care and keeping? It only makes sense.

Psalm 37 makes it clear that David wasn't enjoying everything he was seeing on his "tour" through life. The actions of evildoers and those who threatened and bullied God's people upset him. It disturbed him that wicked people spread their shadows across the land and seemed to prosper. But in the end, He decided to fully trust the Lord. He decided to commit his way to the Lord and wait for Him to act.

> Commit your way to the LORD,
> Trust also in Him,
> And He shall bring it to pass.
> He shall bring forth your righteousness as the light.
> And your justice as the noonday.
> (Psalm 37:5–6)

So, like David, you go to bed at night and commit your way to Him. What can you anticipate? What can you really expect?

What do you hear Him whisper as you drift into sleep?

You can expect and be assured of this: If the Lord gives you another day of life, then as surely as the sun comes up in the morning, He's going to be working to bring about your righteousness and the judgment for which your heart longs. He's going to be working out all the details, and His eyes won't miss a single thing. He won't overlook your faithful trust in Him— and He won't overlook those who walk in pride and arrogance and seek to do you harm.

David had been anxious and fretting over the apparent triumph of the greedy and wicked. He was troubled by all the wrong he saw. But he heard the Lord telling him, "David, do you remember when you were a shepherd boy and watched the sun come up over the hills of Judah? Well, David, as surely as the sun comes up in the east, I'll vindicate your righteousness and will bring things into balance and judgment. Turn loose of that weight you are carrying, and entrust it to Me."

In Psalm 55, it sounds as though David learned that lesson well. He wrote:

Cast your cares on the LORD
and he will sustain you;
he will never let the righteous fall.
(Psalm 55:22, NIV)

In all his trials and tribulations, the apostle Peter must have remembered those words of King David. Peter wrote to a flock of persecuted believers about "casting all your care upon Him, for He cares for you" (1 Peter 5:7).

The word Peter used for *care* literally means *to divide the mind*. Have you ever felt that way? Have you ever felt as though your mind is going in a thousand directions, worrying about so many things that you can't even keep track of them all? You're worried about the past—things you wish you could undo, but can't. You're worried about the present—everything that's going

on in your life right now, making it seem like a three-ring circus. You're worried about the future—you see clouds stacking up on the dark horizon, and you wonder what storms might come sweeping down on you and your family. You wake up in the morning with so many things to do that you feel like crawling right back under your blankets.

Peter says, "Take all of that and cast it on to the Lord." Why? Because He really cares for you. He really cares about everything that happens in your life. He loves you!

David's son Solomon must have learned of this approach to life at his dad's knee. After Solomon assumed his father's throne and became king of Israel, he wrote these words: "Commit to the LORD whatever you do, and your plans will succeed" (Proverbs 16:3, NIV).

How true it was for Solomon! As long as he trusted wholly in the God of his father, his plans *did* succeed—and what great plans they were! He became wise beyond measure, wealthy beyond counting, and esteemed and honored all over the world. But when he turned away from the Lord and began trusting in his own wisdom and worshiping other gods, his plans didn't succeed at all. He led his whole nation into brokenness and disaster.

The truth is: God longs for us to commit our way to Him. He longs for us to trust Him with all of our heart.

HE HELPS ME HELP HIM

I remember hearing a story about a little boy who was helping his father move books out of an attic office into more spacious quarters downstairs. It was important to the little guy that he was helping his dad, even though he was probably getting in the way and slowing things down more than he was actually assisting. But that boy had a wise and patient father who knew that it was more important to work at a task with his young son than it was to move a pile of books efficiently.

Among this man's books were some rather large study

books, and it was a chore for the boy to get them down the stairs. As a matter of fact, on one particular load, the boy dropped his pile of books several times. Finally, he sat down on the stairs and wept in frustration. He wasn't doing any good at all. He wasn't strong enough to carry big books down a narrow stairway. It hurt him to think he couldn't do this for his daddy.

Without a word, the father picked up the dropped load of books, put them back into his boy's arms, and scooped up both the boy and the books into his arms and carried them down the stairs. And so they continued for load after load, enjoying each other's company very much. The boy carried books; the dad carried the boy.

In the same way, God wants to carry you *and* your burdens. And He will, if you commit your way to Him. As sure as the sun comes up in the morning, He'll meet your every need.

CHAPTER TEN

"Rest in Me"

Rest in the LORD, and wait patiently for Him.

PSALM 37:7

Network anchor Dan Rather was a little out of his depth in a television interview with the late Mother Teresa.

Somehow, all of his standard approaches and formula questions were inadequate for the task, and the little nun from Calcutta, sitting beside him so sweetly and tranquilly, didn't seem inclined to make his task easier.

"When you pray," asked Rather, "what do you say to God?"

"I don't say anything," she replied. "I listen."

Rather tried another tack. "Well, okay...when God speaks to you, then, what does He say?"

"He doesn't say anything. He listens."

Rather looked bewildered. For an instant, he didn't know what to say.

"And if you don't understand that," Mother Teresa added, "I can't explain it to you."

Did this good woman mean she never said words to God? I don't think so. I would imagine she prayed rather actively for her work of mercy in the streets and alleys of Calcutta. I think

she was trying to make the point to a seasoned television celebrity that prayer is something more than repeating certain phrases or formulas. Prayer is more than an elaborate construction of pious-sounding words.

Prayer is the intimate communication between two hearts…yours and God's. Prayer is letting Him feel what's on your heart, and He, in turn, letting you feel what's on His.

You don't necessarily need words for that transaction. But you do need to understand what the Bible says about rest.

"HOLD THEE STILL!"

The word that David uses for *rest* in Psalm 37 is rich with meaning. In a literal sense, it means to be mute, like an individual incapable of speech. In a broader sense, it implies both quiet submission and patient waiting.

When you rest before God, you must decide in your heart that He is in control—whether life circumstances are going your way or not. To rest, you must leave everything in His hands and wait for Him to make things right.

At times, David came before the Lord with an offended sense of justice at the way things were turning out in his world. He didn't like the headlines. He didn't like what he saw up and down his land. How could people be so hard and cruel? So heartless? How could they trample innocent people the way they did? How could they be so arrogant and conceited? Who did they think they were? It was maddening to think about! It really got to him.

It gets to all of us sometimes, doesn't it?

It's enough to keep you awake at night. The unkindness. The casual cruelty. The malicious gossip. The unfair advantage. The broken commitments. The lies. The betrayals of trust. The thoughtless snubs. The deliberate hurts.

Sometimes we feel so angry, and then afterwards, when the anger burns away, we're left with the ashes of emptiness and depression.

In Psalm 37, David urges us to set all those things aside and to come before the Lord. He invites us into an attitude of open-handed quietness before God.

Writing about this verse, Charles H. Spurgeon said, "Hold thee still!" In other words, don't move, don't speak, don't try to explain or argue, don't murmur about your situation. Rest says, "I'm not going to complain about where I am and how I'm doing—or about how others might be doing in comparison to me. I'm going to be silent. I'll just rest here, believing in my heart that my heavenly Father will do what's best."

"BE EASY, SON...."

I'm normally very occupied and as busy as I can be as pastor of a large fellowship—sometimes I'm on the run seven days a week. Being a shepherd to these wonderful people is an incredible privilege and the very joy of my life. I love seeing this flock fed and cared for. It's a big task, much bigger than I am, but the Lord enables, and I'm passionate about it.

After a severe heart attack a number of years ago, I had no idea what was going to happen to my ministry. During my recuperation, I found myself lying in bed in a quiet room, too weary to talk or even think. I knew the Lord was there. It wasn't that I was always thinking about Him—I just sensed His presence. I wanted to communicate with Him, but I didn't know what to say. Somehow, I couldn't form the words.

But even in that fog of weariness and weakness, I could sense the Lord telling me, "Be easy, son. You don't have to say anything."

He already knew what was going on in my spirit. He knew how I felt. He knew what I had been through and what I was going through. He knew the drifting, shapeless concerns I couldn't form into sentences. *What will I do? Am I ever going to pastor again? Will I get to go back to the church? How severe was the damage? Will the Lord take me home soon? What will Joyce and the boys do? Will they be all right?*

I knew it wasn't time to ask such questions. That would come later. For now, it was enough just to be quiet before Him, to be in His presence and wait on Him. I didn't need to explain anything to Him, and He didn't need to explain anything to me. I didn't need to know why or how or when, and I didn't want or expect Him to tell me. We just spent time together, enjoying each other's nearness. I knew that my life was in His hands, whether I lived or died, whether I ever got up from that bed or not, whether I ever preached again or not. It was up to Him, and knowing how much He loves me, I could rest in that. In His time, I would know what I needed to know.

It will be that way with us sometimes. There will be times when we are so troubled in heart or confused or grieved that we simply won't have any words. There will be times when we can't think of anything to say to Him and when He doesn't seem to be saying anything to us.

In times like those, God would have us simply quiet ourselves in His presence and rest—rest in His constant love, His faithfulness, and His cleansing and forgiveness. Rest in the mighty refuge of who He is and in the fact that all will be well.

A FATHER WHO IS THERE

I can remember times as my boys were growing up when one of them was very troubled or worried or had endured a disappointment or hurt. Sometimes after he was in bed at night, I'd go and just lie down on the bed beside him. It's nice if you can think of wise, fatherly words in those moments, but the words aren't always there. It was enough just to lie beside my boy and be there with him.

In the old TV shows, like *Leave It to Beaver* and *Father Knows Best,* the dad (usually in a jacket and tie) would sit on his child's bed and say all kinds of profound, memorable things. But that's Hollywood. In real life, the words aren't always there when you want them. But you can still *be there.* You can still be close. You can still be a comfort and a compan-

ion by your very proximity. Your simple presence says, "I'm with you in this. I care about how you feel. I wish there was something I could do to help. I'm so sorry you're hurting. I love you very much."

Was that a trouble or bother for me to do, to lie beside my sons like that? Of course not! It was a high privilege. When you love someone, you enjoy being with him or her. You like being close. You cherish sharing that time, even if neither of you has a word to say. With all my heart, I wanted to be the kind of dad who took advantage of those priceless times.

And the Lord wants to be that kind of a Father to you—a Father who is there and who is active, not passive, toward you. He *likes* you. He chooses to be near you. He has a trillion solar systems to run and galaxies beyond number to guide through the heavens. He has a lot of important places to be and people to meet and things to do...but He especially likes just to spend time—quiet time—with you.

"Cease Striving"

In Psalm 46:10, the Lord says: "Be still, and know that I am God." Another translation says: "Cease striving and know that I am God" (NASB).

Have you taken time for that in your life in recent days? Have you come into His presence and, without saying a word, taken time to consider *who He is?* How can you really do that when you come rushing into His presence with your heart full of worries and strife and your mouth full of complaints and fears?

"Be still!" He says. "Hush. Cease striving. Do you know who I am? I am God. I am the Creator and Lord of the universe. I am the One who is all-powerful and all-knowing. I am the One who has always been and always will be. I am the One for whom nothing is impossible. I am above time; I live in eternity. And I am the One who sent My own Son from My side to buy you back from the kingdom of darkness and the slave market of sin."

Be still. Set your worries aside. Put your petitions down. File your complaints for a while. Tuck your long list of requests in your pocket. *Think* for a minute about this One you wish to speak to.

In the little, frequently overlooked book of Zephaniah, the prophet speaks of a future day when Israel will enjoy with a full heart the nearness of God.

> "The LORD your God in your midst,
> The Mighty One, will save;
> He will rejoice over you with gladness,
> He will quiet you in His love,
> He will rejoice over you with singing."
> (Zephaniah 3:17)

Those are the kind of moments God wants to share with all of His children—if we would give Him the opportunity.

"COME WITH ME BY YOURSELVES...."

When I was dating Joyce in Bible college, I would find ways to be with her. I wanted to eat lunch when she ate lunch. I wanted to walk to class when she walked to class. Whatever her off-campus ministry was, I wanted to do the same thing. I changed majors to be in more classes with her. I changed churches to keep her close on Sundays. I didn't want her to have the opportunity to discover she could get along without me!

Jesus planned times to be with His disciples, too. They walked long distances together. They sailed across the Sea of Galilee on an evening wind. They ate together on sunny hillsides. They slept in ancient olive groves under even more ancient starlight. At one point, when the schedule was getting too harried and the pressure was growing too heavy, He said: "Come with me by yourselves to a quiet place and get some rest" (Mark 6:31, NIV).

Isn't that a beautiful invitation? Wouldn't you love to go back in time and take the Lord Jesus up on that offer? Can you imagine just sitting with Him under a tree on the banks of the Jordan? Can't you imagine just resting with Him there, knowing that you are completely loved and completely secure in the presence of God's mighty Son?

Are you giving the Lord the opportunity to speak to you even here and now? Are you allowing yourself to rest?

The truth is, you will never enjoy rest until you've finished your work. My mom, tired as she may have been, would never have climbed into bed if dirty dishes were still in the sink. She wouldn't have been able to sleep, knowing that her work wasn't done.

What is our work? Our first work, as Jesus said, is to believe on the One whom God has sent (John 6:28–29). If we are to receive forgiveness of sins and eternal salvation, we must put our trust in the finished work of Jesus Christ on the cross.

But in the context of Psalm 37, what is our work? What is God asking us, through the psalmist, to do? David has the answer: "Don't fret.... Trust in the Lord.... Delight yourself in the Lord.... Commit your way to the Lord."

Then—when you've finally turned to Him with all your heart and entrusted every troubling fragment of your life to Him—you will find rest. If you are still going to bed restless and troubled at night—if you are still turning the issues and worries of your life around and around in your thoughts as you lie in bed—you haven't finished your work. You won't be able to rest.

What a blessed sense of relief and release we feel when we truly understand and acknowledge that all of life is in His hands. From birth to death, from the turbulent teen years to the equally turbulent passage through midlife, from sunny childhood to the shadows of advanced old age, He is there. And if you allow Him, He will carry you all the way.

Through Isaiah, the Lord said to Israel:

"Listen to me, O house of Jacob...
you whom I have upheld since you were conceived,
and have carried since your birth.
Even to your old age and gray hairs
I am he, I am he who will sustain you.
I have made you and I will carry you;
I will sustain you and I will rescue you."
(Isaiah 46:3–4, NIV)

I heard once about a dear, saintly old woman who was gradually losing her memory. Details began to blur. Once-familiar names began to elude her, and finally, even well-loved faces slipped from recognition. Throughout her life, however, this woman had cherished and depended on the Word of God, committing to memory many verses from her worn King James Bible.

Her favorite verse had always been 2 Timothy 1:12: "For I know whom I have believed and am persuaded that He is able to keep what I have committed to Him until that Day."

Finally, she was confined to bed in a nursing home, and her family knew that she would never leave the bed alive. As they visited with her, she would still occasionally quote verses of Scripture, especially 2 Timothy 1:12. But with the passing of time, even parts of this well-loved verse began to slip away.

"I know whom I have believed," she would say, "He is able to keep...what I have committed...to Him."

Her voice grew weaker. And the verse became even shorter. "What I have committed...to Him."

As she was dying, her voice became so faint that family members had to bend over to hear the few whispered words on her lips. And at the end, there was only one word of her life left:

"Him."

She whispered it again and again as she stood on the threshold of heaven. "Him...Him...Him."

It was all that was left. It was all that was needed. She couldn't recall the verse, but the word she remembered was by far the most important word in the Bible. She held onto the one word that is really the heart of the Word—"Him."

Real peace and rest is all about Him.

CHAPTER ELEVEN

"Wait on Me"

Wait patiently for Him.

PSALM 37:7

*B*lair Martini couldn't remember her dad. Marc had died unexpectedly when she was just a baby.

But she had seen his pictures. She'd seen the photos of him cradling her, looking down at her with adoring eyes. Sometimes it *seemed* as though she could remember him, and she loved him with all the loyal intensity of a nine-year-old girl.

Last Valentine's Day, Blair made cards for the special people in her life. (Trust me, her cards are very pretty.) If her dad had been living, Blair would have taken paper, scissors, and crayons and made him a card to tell him how much she loved him.

Couldn't she *still* make a Valentine for him?

She asked her mom, Patty, who thought about it for a moment. Yes, she said quietly, Blair could do that if she wanted to. And Blair did want to, very much. So they went to the store together, and the little girl picked out what she needed for the task.

Blair sat down at the kitchen table with all her things and

made her card, taking her usual care to make it very special. When she was done, she solemnly asked her mom for a helium-filled balloon. That was a bit of a surprise, and Patty really didn't understand. But sensing this was important to Blair, she found one—a red one—and brought it home.

Blair carefully taped her card to the balloon and went out to the backyard. Patty followed, watching her little girl walk around and around, looking for an open patch of sky, free of tree branches and power lines. She didn't want anything to hinder the balloon's flight.

Hand in hand, Patty and Blair watched the red balloon sweep up into the blue winter sky. It became tinier and tinier, until it was a dot the size of a pinhead. And then it was gone.

Blair said, "Mom, I hope he gets the message."

She knew very well that she would see her daddy again someday. Her mother had given her a verse from the Bible and told her that even though Daddy couldn't come to where they were, they could go to where he was (2 Samuel 12:23).

But they would have to wait. Perhaps a very long time.

Blair understood the waiting part. But in the meantime she wanted to send her dad the message that she would be coming along as soon as she could.

WAITING WITH HOPE

I think Blair understands the word *wait* in the way David used it in Psalm 37. And I think it's a word that God would whisper to us frequently in those dark and trying times of life.

When David used the word in verses 7 and 34, he wasn't using it the way we sometimes do. When we talk about waiting, we get it all mixed up with thoughts of boredom, impatience, or wasting time.

Most Americans hate even the thought of waiting. We will change lines in a grocery store three times to find the fastest checker (only to have him or her go on a break just when we step up to the register). We will change lanes or pass to get

around a slow driver. On an escalator, we'll walk around people who have the nerve just to stand there. We feel tense or upset if someone doesn't show up on time.

Those are our thoughts about waiting.

But they were not David's.

When David used the word, he was thinking about *hope*. He was talking about looking for something with longing and eager expectation. In Psalm 37, David is eagerly waiting for God to deliver and reward the righteous, while dispensing judgment to the wicked. He is waiting for God to bring justice, and he expects it soon.

A friend of mine relates a childhood memory about his little cousin who, after staying at his grandparents' house for several days, was waiting for his mom and dad to pick him up. The homesick boy sat in the old swivel rocker all morning, staring and staring out the picture window. From that window, he could see down the long, gravel road. He was watching for that telltale cloud of dust that would signal the approach of the family car.

After a couple of hours of this, the grandfather came by and said in mock exasperation, "Doggone it, Bill, you're gonna stare a hole right through our window!"

Bill knew who was coming that morning. And he expected to see that cloud of dust and the familiar blue and white '54 Ford station wagon roll up at any moment. He had no desire to play outside or even move from that chair. He focused all his energies and attention on that long, empty road.

Waiting with Intensity

Have you ever been in a situation like that—when you were waiting and waiting with all your might?

Perhaps it was late at night on the curb at an airport terminal. Drained and exhausted from your travels, you fervently longed for nothing more than to fall into bed. The hotel told you that the courtesy van was on the way—but so was Christmas! It was taking so long. You looked and looked and

waited and waited. Every car or bus or van that came around the corner had your earnest, eager attention.

Or maybe you've been at a crowded airport gate, looking and waiting for that one well-loved face among the sea of strangers getting off the plane.

The psalmist wrote:

I wait for the LORD, my soul waits,
and in his word I put my hope.
My soul waits for the Lord
more than watchmen wait for the morning,
more than watchmen wait for the morning.
(Psalm 130:5–6, NIV)

Being a sentry on the wall of a city was a tiresome, lonely job. (Ask any security guard or night watchman.) The weary sentries on top of the wall of Jerusalem walked back and forth, wondering if the long night would ever end. At every turn, they looked off toward the eastern horizon, waiting for even the slightest indication of the approaching dawn. Did the darkness seem the tiniest bit less dense? Was there the slightest hint of gray, low in the horizon? Wasn't that dark clump of palm trees alongside the wall becoming just a little more distinct? Wasn't that a rooster crowing, somewhere in the distance?

How they longed for morning! And the psalmist said, "That's how it is for me, as I wait for the Lord. I've put all my hope in Him. I'm eagerly anticipating His touch on my life."

It's that expectation that sustains you in the times of darkness. It's that knowledge that the waiting will soon be over. Dawn will arrive, and your desires will be fulfilled.

Waiting with eager expectation is an entirely different proposition from just plain waiting. Do you know what makes all the difference in waiting?

It's knowing for whom you are waiting!

When you think about the word *wait,* please don't think

about sitting in the lobby of a dentist's office waiting for your name to be called. Think about little Blair waiting through the tears and the years to see her daddy again. Think about a groom, standing at the altar, waiting for his bride to come down the aisle—waiting for that blessed new life together that is now so near!

WORTH WAITING FOR

Centuries after King David penned Psalm 37, the prophet Isaiah also wrote about waiting, and I think he understood the word the way Blair and David did. "Those who wait on the LORD," he wrote, "shall renew their strength" (Isaiah 40:31).

Do you know why that familiar verse comes near the end of Isaiah chapter 40? It's because he spent the first thirty verses describing exactly who it is we're waiting for!

- He is a God who revealed Himself in Christ—and who will reveal Himself yet again. (vv. 3–5)
- He is a God whose Word stands forever. (vv. 6–8)
- He is a God who will one day rule our poor, bruised planet with a strong, righteous hand and will reward His own beyond imagination. (v. 10)
- He is a God who guards and cares for His lambs like a tenderhearted shepherd. (v. 11)
- He is a God so big that He measured the heavens with His hand, named every star in the countless galaxies of the universe, and now directs their fiery courses through the pathways of space. (vv. 12, 26)
- He is a God who has all knowledge and complete wisdom. (vv. 13–14)
- He is a God who never overlooks our needs, becomes weary, or fails to note and understand our heart's desires. (vv. 27–28)
- He is a God who gives power to the weak and strength to the weary. (vv. 29–30)

So as you spend time together in the darkness, if you hear Him whisper the word *wait,* don't let it throw you. If anyone was *ever* worth waiting for, He is.

The reason we can wait on God is because we know the conclusion of all things. We'll be safe and gloriously happy with our Lord forever! No, we don't know everything that will happen in between, but we know the end. God will see us through. He'll make a way—just as He always does.

By the way, if you happen to find a red balloon with a very fancy but somewhat weathered card taped to it, please forward it. A little girl named Blair is waiting with eager expectation to see her Valentine again—and so she will.

In the long run, the wait won't be very long at all.

CHAPTER TWELVE

"Your Pain Has a Purpose"

*E*ven in the merry old Land of Oz, it seemed that everyone on his or her way to the Emerald City wanted something different. Every traveler on that storied Yellow Brick Road yearned for some essential quality or possession to change his or her life situation.

The scarecrow sensed the need for a brain in his burlap noggin.

The tin man begged for a heart to fill his empty chest.

The cowardly lion longed for a big dose of courage to steady his knocking knees.

And Dorothy? She didn't ask for too much—just a plane ticket home to Kansas!

This is one of those children's stories that somehow manages to make a significant statement about grown-up life. Everybody, it seems, wants to experience some kind of change or transformation in life. In my office, I talk to people all the time who desperately seek that "big change" that will bring relief or help, deliverance or happiness to their lives. We all want the sort of change that brings us a sense of peace and a settled calm in these turbulent days.

The pathway to real life change, however, may not be

peaceful at all. More often than not, it leads over rough, rocky—even perilous—ground.

The Rough Path to Change

God is committed to moving you and me from a position of personal weakness to one of enduring strength in Him.

His ongoing, never-ceasing plan is to conform each of His children into the very image of His dear Son. Romans 8:29 makes that very clear:

> From the very beginning God decided that those who came to him—and all along he knew who would—should become like his Son, so that his Son would be the First, with many brothers." (TLB)

That's the one thing—the big thing—He's always about through all our days, no matter where we are, no matter what we're experiencing. His unchanging will for our lives is that we become more and more like Jesus.

Even so, I've found myself wondering at times how such change can really happen. You know what I mean. You begin thinking that someone in your circle of acquaintance—or perhaps your own family—will simply never change. In fact, you may be thinking that very thing about your own life! You see those weak and vulnerable areas—places where you've stumbled so often—and begin to despair. You feel as if you've only been going around in circles, and you wonder if it will ever be any different.

In such times, I've been encouraged to remember Hebrews 11:34, which describes those people of faith who "out of weakness were made strong."

Now there's a phrase that lifts my spirits!

Here were weak people like you and me who, for whatever reason, really longed to see change in their lives, and through faith in God, they *found* it! It truly happened. Out of their

weakness, their inadequacies, their limitations, their diminished resources, the Lord changed them and made them into something mighty.

Notice that it doesn't say, "Out of weakness they were made a little better" or "Out of weakness they were made average." No, God took them from faintness and frailty to a position of significant strength in Him. The term *strong* in this verse is based on *dunamis,* the potent Greek word for power. It's also the word from which we get our term *dynamite!*

Maybe you feel as though you are in a particularly weak and vulnerable time in your life. Because of health, family circumstances, or failing finances, you're afraid that the next little puff of wind might push you right off your feet. I believe that the same strength-out-of-weakness principle holds true. Out of the most devastating circumstances, in the shakiest time you can ever remember, He can pour into your life strength beyond anything you've ever experienced. Out of this weakness, this time of darkness and adversity, He can change your life and make you a stronger, more secure man or woman.

UNLIKELY WARRIOR

Where does God find His mighty soldiers of the faith?

It isn't necessarily in the Marine Corps or the graduating class of West Point. As a matter of fact, Judges 6 tells us that heaven's recruitment office finds its best candidates in some rather unorthodox places.

> The angel of the LORD came and sat down under the oak in Ophrah that belonged to Joash the Abiezrite, where his son Gideon was threshing wheat in a winepress to keep it from the Midianites. When the angel of the LORD appeared to Gideon, he said, "The LORD is with you, mighty warrior." (vv. 11–12, NIV)

Many believe that Gideon's visitor, described as "the angel of the LORD," was none other than God's Son appearing in human form. One commentator pictures the Lord arriving at the small winepress under the oak tree, staff in hand, dressed as a common traveler taking rest in the shade.[1]

"Mighty warrior"? What could the Lord have meant? Gideon was crouching in a winepress under a sheltering tree, trying to thresh a little grain out of sight of the Midianites. If ever he felt humiliated and powerless, that was the time. If ever he sensed a weak and defenseless time in his nation's history, it had to be right then. And yet...

> The LORD turned to him and said, "Go in the strength you have and save Israel out of Midian's hand. Am I not sending you?" (v. 14, NIV)

Strength? What strength? Gideon had none. Even in his own eyes, he was the least likely hero he could think of.

> "But Lord," Gideon asked, "how can I save Israel? My clan is the weakest in Manasseh, and I am the least in my family." (v. 15, NIV)
> The LORD answered, "I will be with you, and you will strike down the Midianites as if they were but one man." (v. 16, NIV)

God was on the move—recruiting weak people in precarious situations to prove His power. As it turned out, Gideon was an ideal candidate for a demonstration of heavenly might. He had nothing to bring to the table—no army, no strength, no experience, no courage, no weapons, no plans, and no clue at all what to do. It was a situation custom-made to exalt the strong arm of Israel's God.

Later, when Gideon had raised a significant (if reluctant) army to fight the invaders, the Lord had him send almost

everybody home! God said to Gideon, "There are too many of you! I can't let all of you fight the Midianites, for then the people of Israel will boast to me that they saved themselves by their own strength! Send home any of your men who are timid and frightened" (Judges 7:2–3, TLB).

So General Gideon ended up with a ragtag band of three hundred warriors—against an enemy force so huge it couldn't even be numbered. And the victory was...easy.

God is still on the move today. He's still recruiting for the army of heaven, and He's still looking for the most improbable of recruits in the most unlikely of places. If you see yourself as a weak individual in impossible circumstances, He's ready to use you in an especially powerful way for His kingdom purposes. And when victory is declared, guess who gets the glory? As a matter of fact, He'll arrange the odds in your life to make sure you understand that it is His power alone, and nothing of your own, that guaranteed the victory.

REFINED LIKE WINE

God is up to something in our lives. He knows the plans He has for us (Jeremiah 29:11), and they are neither small nor insignificant. He wants our lives to be full and abundant (John 10:10), and He wants us to experience the mighty heights and depths of His love and provision (Ephesians 3:17–20). Because of those things, He's committed to bringing change into our lives, no matter what the cost.

Yes, there is a price tag. And it's that "cost" part we don't like, isn't it? We dread and shrink away from those dark times that fall on our lives—those days and nights when we feel pressed out of measure and in way over our heads.

We don't like those difficult experiences. Yet God knows there may be no other path that will deliver us from gray mediocrity or bondage to life-sapping habits and inclinations. Passing through a gloomy tunnel of pain and pressure, we (finally) emerge to realize that we've begun to grow in Jesus

Christ. After all, the question isn't just, "Am I changing?" It's *"Who am I becoming?"* If I continually resist God's process of change—if I insist on forging ahead in my own chosen rut—I *will* reap the results of those decisions. How much better to face up to a couple of uncomfortable questions right now—questions such as, "What will my life be like in five or ten years if I keep going this way? What kind of person will I have become?"

The answers may not be happy thoughts to contemplate.

In the book of Jeremiah, God gives a graphic word picture of stagnation in the little nation of Moab. The Lord told the prophet, "Moab has been at rest from youth, like wine left on its dregs, not poured from one jar to another—she has not gone into exile. So she tastes as she did, and her aroma is unchanged" (Jeremiah 48:11, NIV).

Moab had been secure and prosperous for generations. Though surrounded by potent neighbors, she remained snug and smug, insulated from the warfare and turmoil all around her. In this biblical word picture, God compared the Moabites to raw wine that is undisturbed, resting on its dregs. The taste always remains just the same because the wine has not been poured from vessel to vessel. In Moab's case, that wasn't good. It had been an evil nation for years and years; hearts and lives were unchanged and unresponsive to the God of Israel.

Adversity stirs us out of our slumbers and changes and refines our lives. In those dark, perplexing seasons—the times when anxiety and pressure seem to camp forever on our doorstep—God wants to draw something out of our lives. Each time we face such circumstances and endure them through faith in the Lord, God draws out just a little bit more of the bitterness, a little bit more of the worry, a little bit more of the self-centeredness, a little bit more of the self-reliance.

The Moabites never changed because they never had to deal with any difficult or challenging times. They were never brought face-to-face with their own helplessness and their stark need for God's help. So instead of being grateful and thankful

to the true and living God for their years of peace and tranquility, they worshiped false gods and became cocky and proud. Israel, however, fought battle after battle, endured adversity after adversity—with Babylonian captivity stretching out ahead of them. God wanted to use those times to separate them from the dregs. He wanted to draw the rebellion and bitterness out of them and bring a sweetness and refinement in its place.

FROM TROUBLE TO TROUBLE

In a little book that chronicles so much personal pain, the apostle Paul writes, "But we all, with unveiled face, beholding as in a mirror the glory of the Lord, are being transformed into the same image from glory to glory, just as by the Spirit of the Lord" (2 Corinthians 3:18).

When Paul speaks of us being changed "from glory to glory," he could just as well be saying *from trouble to trouble...from challenge to challenge...from trial to trial.* Why? Because in the midst of my struggles, in the midst of my weakness and helplessness to change, God's glory rests upon me as I trust in Him. So every time I face a time of trouble, darkness, or hardship, I experience just a little more of His glory in my life. I am changed, and He begins to use me in new and wonderful ways.

What was Paul's response to all this stress and perplexity? "Therefore I will boast all the more gladly about my weaknesses, so that Christ's power may rest on me. That is why, for Christ's sake, I delight in weaknesses, in insults, in hardships, in persecutions, in difficulties. For when I am weak, then I am strong" (2 Corinthians 12:9–10, NIV).

When do I experience the greatest surge of Christ's power in my life? It is when I acknowledge my points of weakness and affirm by faith that God will make me strong in those very areas. I guess it all boils down to two simple essentials for life change: His commitment to bring it about and my willingness to let Him do it!

Those "glory to glory" times of change—uncomfortable as they may be—are good for us because we get to see God at work. We get to see what He's going to do in the midst of it all. It's an opportunity for us to realize afresh that God is preparing us for something ahead—He's equipping us for the challenges we'll face next week, next month, or next year. He knows very well what will cross our path in the coming days, so He's doing a work in our hearts now to prepare us. It's humbling because all of us must come to the realization that we can't change without God's help. We have to trust His individualized program for our lives.

When somebody tells you about how smooth and easy his life has been—with green lights and sunny days all along the way—don't let yourself become envious. He may be living in Moab. He may be the kind of person about whom the Lord says, "You never went through anything. So the bitterness remains in your life. You will live in the dregs of your complacency."

Do you remember how *The Wizard of Oz* concludes? The mighty wizard is revealed as a bumbling fake—a cheap charlatan—with no power to help anybody. Dorothy finally gets home, only to discover that her journey had been nothing more than a dream.

But we have a sovereign God who will provide us with everything we need for life in the real world. He's the One who dispenses intelligence and wisdom when we need it. He's the One who gives us tender compassion when our supplies have run dry. He's the One who gives us courage to face the hazards of the road, though our journey be long and steep. Finally, Philippians 1:6 reminds us that He has begun a good work in our lives and that He'll never cease. He'll never stop bringing about positive changes until He brings us all the way home.

And I don't mean to Kansas.

1. Jamieson, Fausset, and Brown Commentary, Electronic Database. © 1997 by Biblesoft.

CHAPTER THIRTEEN

"Taste My Joy"

*R*ub-a-dub-dub, three Ortbergs in the tub.

John Ortberg had his hands full bathing his three little ones, Laura, Johnny, and Mallory. An efficient man, he bathed them all at once to save time. He knew it was a situation that wouldn't last forever; before long, three at a time wouldn't work at all. In the back of his mind, this harried dad probably realized he'd someday look back on these times with his small children as a privilege.

At the moment, however....

It was hard to keep his patience as he scrubbed those three slippery little seals. I can imagine him ending up sopping wet, kneeling in a pool of sloshed water and suds on the bathroom floor.

Laura was always first out, first to be toweled, and first to run daintily down the hall to climb into her pajamas. Johnny liked to take his time (probably reluctant to leave his imaginary sea battles), but eventually he scrambled out of the tub and headed for his room and his Ninja pajamas.

Then came Mallory.

Mallory was always last. Tired and on the edge of his endurance, John would extract the little maid from the tub and

attempt to towel her dry. But Mallory didn't want to be dry. Mallory didn't want to get dressed.

Mallory wanted to dance.

The littlest Ortberg would twirl and pirouette like a ballerina. She would squiggle and wiggle and sing, "It's a Dee-Dah Day!"

On one particular night, John's frustration got the better of him. "Mallory, *hurry!*" he barked at the dancing mermaid. Mallory danced faster! "No, Mallory, that's not what I mean! Stop with the dee-dah day stuff, and get over here so I can dry you off. Hurry!"

The little girl looked at him with wide eyes.

"Why?" she asked.

John opened his mouth to reply—but then realized he really didn't have an answer. He had nowhere to go, nothing to do, no meetings to attend, no sermons to write. And why *shouldn't* his little girl dance and sing and be happy?

Later, he reflected: *I spend most of my life in transit—trying to get somewhere, waiting to begin, driving someplace, standing in line, waiting for a meeting to end, trying to get a task completed, worrying about something bad that might happen, or being angry about something that did happen.*

Drying off the kids that night was just one more thing he was hurrying to *get through*. He had allowed circumstances to make him feel hurried, troubled, and tense. It had become a habit of life. A grim, grit-your-teeth attitude had edged joy right out of his life—though it danced like sunlight outside shuttered windows.[1]

The little jitterbug named Mallory couldn't imagine any day that wasn't a "dee-dah day." And the truth is, she was a lot closer to God's will on that score than her uptight dad was.

The apostle Paul never wrote about "dee-dah days," per se, but he was as specific as could be when it came to commanding joy in the Christian life.

Finally, my brothers, rejoice in the Lord! …Rejoice in the Lord always. I will say it again: Rejoice! (Philippians 3:1; 4:4, NIV)

Be joyful always; pray continually; give thanks in all circumstances, for this is God's will for you in Christ Jesus. (1 Thessalonians 5:16–18, NIV)

The only way I know how to live in the reality of these verses—to rejoice all the time, no matter what—is to let your mind dwell on God. People who remain calm and peaceful in the midst of difficult circumstances have a perspective about God that others don't. So many people spend their days looking for quick fixes and Band-Aid solutions to their problems, running everywhere looking for an answer, looking for experiences that will bring a moment or two of happiness.

In commanding joy, Paul never said it would come easy. But you could never accuse the battered apostle of neglecting to practice what he so consistently preached.

In Acts 16, Luke says that Paul and Silas suffered a horrendous beating at the hands of the city fathers of Philippi. Bruised, bleeding from dozens of open wounds, and wracked with awful pain, they were locked away in an inner dungeon. This would have been a damp, cold place, where chains rusted on the prisoners' wrists and ankles. The jailer took the further precaution of fastening their feet in stocks—an instrument of torture as well as confinement. It was midnight in that dismal little cell, and pitch dark. The pain was savage.

Just the right time for a praise chorus or two, wouldn't you say?

MUSIC IN THE DUNGEON

Can you imagine the conversation preceding that little praise rally in the Philippi City Jail?

Silas tries to change his position—difficult to do, when your feet are bound in stocks—and groans with pain.

"Silas?" Paul whispers. "Silas, are you okay? Is there anything I can do?"

"I'm all right. I'll live, I guess. How about you?"

"I don't think any bones are broken."

"That's a plus, I guess. Man! My back feels like it's on fire."

"Yeah. Flogging will do that to you. I hurt like crazy. All over."

"Paul?"

"Yes?"

"What do you think they're gonna do?"

"I don't know, my friend, but it doesn't look good."

"Do you think...this is the end?"

"Could be."

"What should we do?"

Paul, a thoughtful man, gives that some consideration. "Well," he begins, "remember what our brothers Peter and John did—back in those days when that first wave of persecution hit the church? When the Jewish leaders flogged them, they praised God that they'd been counted worthy to suffer for the sake of the Name. We could do that."

"You mean, just start praising God? Right now? Out loud?"

"Why not?" Paul grins ruefully in the dark. "What have we got to lose?"

And so they did. It began with a hoarse whisper and rose to a mighty shout as their joy increased. Soon, they were singing favorite hymns in two-part harmony, full-throated and joyous, in the bowels of that dark place.

Why did they sing? Because they knew that God was going to send an earthquake and open the prison doors for them?

No, I don't think they had any idea what God was going to do. Paul and Silas sang expecting nothing. They simply rejoiced because they belonged to the Lord. They sang because they knew their God worked in the dark and that nothing could stand in the way of His purposes.

"AND THE OTHER PRISONERS WERE LISTENING...."

The two missionaries may have been in a maximum-security lockup, but the facility wasn't soundproof! Their hymns and prayers drifted along those dark, smelly corridors. The other inmates heard—and must have been stunned by what they were hearing.

Weren't these the men who had just been beaten and placed in stocks? What was this music? What were these words about the greatness of God, the majesty of His name, and the tenderness of His mercies?

The wounded men sang, and others took note of their song. They rejoiced, and their rejoicing touched lives.

It's the same for you and me. Never doubt it! No matter what you may be enduring, there are those who will watch and listen to see how you handle it. You may never even realize you're being observed. It may be the student nurse in the hospital who takes your blood pressure. It may be your retired neighbor who overhears conversations in your backyard. It may be a coworker who seems to take no notice of you at all. It may be the teacher at school who talks to your children. It doesn't really matter who it is. If there's a song in your heart, when by all reason and logic, there shouldn't be, people will listen—and wonder what makes the difference in your life.

But your praise in the darkness not only touches other people, it also touches the heart of God. And He will not remain idle during such times. He will come to you as He came to Paul and Silas that night in Philippi. When He hears your sacrifice of praise through gray days of pressure or long nights of loneliness and pain, He will do something. I'm not

saying that He will immediately open your prison doors or unleash an earthquake, but I believe that your song will activate something in the Almighty, releasing Him to minister in and through you in some fresh and effective way.

A song in the dark is powerful.

A song rising out of sorrow soars like no other.

THE UGLIEST, MOST BEAUTIFUL SONG

A few years ago, I was invited to Taiwan to speak to missionaries and national leaders from thirty-five countries in Asia. What a humbling experience that was for me! I spoke to them a number of times over the course of several days, but I think the most memorable and touching moment for me was at communion, sharing the bread and the cup with men who had once worn bones in their noses and with women who had tattooed faces.

During the service, several people gave testimonies. Then one man rose to sing. I don't know what I had been expecting when he opened his mouth—maybe some soft, soothing rendition of "Break Thou the Bread of Life." I certainly wasn't prepared for what followed.

It was the most atrocious attempt at singing I had ever heard in my life. I couldn't believe my ears. I thought, *This guy must have the worst voice in the world.* Whatever his listeners may have thought of his song, the man took no notice. With lifted face and eyes streaming with tears, he kept right on singing—if you could call it that.

I'll admit it, I was embarrassed. I kept thinking, *How could you be that bad and even want to stand up there by yourself and sing?*

As if he were reading my thoughts, my friend leaned over and said, "Ron, do you know anything about this man?"

"No."

"He's a pastor...and one of the most courageous men I've ever met. He's been imprisoned, beaten again and again, even bayoneted in the chest for preaching Christ. He's lost everything he ever had. He shouldn't even be alive, but he is. And

he's still preaching. Nothing can silence him."

Sobered, I asked, "Well, what's he singing, anyway?"

"He's singing, 'I'll never turn back,'" my friend told me. "He's saying, 'I'll never quit, I'll never give up.'"

I looked back at the man singing and said, "This is the prettiest song I've ever heard in my life."

You see, it is the *context* of our praise that speaks even more powerfully than the words themselves. Anyone can sing after winning the lottery, getting straight A's, or watching the high school volleyball team clinch the city championship. Frankly, no one pays much attention to that kind of rejoicing. People *expect* it. But after the roof has caved in on your life, and someone walks by the plaster and rubble and hears music coming from under the fallen rafters—*then* your song becomes a thing of power.

If you're finding it difficult to bless and thank the Lord at this particular time in your life, let me suggest just a few things I've been learning that help keep me on track:

- I'm learning that, from early in the morning until late at night, the Lord provides for those who put their trust in Him.
- I'm learning that when I let the Lord be concerned about tomorrow, I can just live for today.
- I'm learning to stand without fear on the promises of God.
- I'm learning to count on the fact that the Lord is *always* in control of my situation.
- I'm learning that no matter how large or impossible the barrier before me, God always makes a way.
- I'm learning that I have access to Him at any time and at all times.

I'm also learning that, strange as it may seem, the happiest people I've ever been around are often those who seemingly have so very little to be happy about.

THE WOMEN WHO DANCED

While I was in Asia, I was invited to speak in a Filipino church in Hong Kong, which I was delighted to do.

When I walked in the door, I noticed two things right away. First, the congregation was mostly female, and second, it was the most joyous worship I had experienced in many years.

Many women in the church were Filipino domestics who worked for wealthy Chinese families. The more I learned about their situation in that city, the more amazed I became at the joy that overflowed that little church. The Filipino women earn very little, and most of what they do earn they send back to their families in the Philippines. Some of these women, I found, work away from their homes and families for up to *five years* at a time. When they do return home, they find children who hardly know them and a husband who may very well be living with another woman.

But you should hear these women sing!

You should experience their worship.

You would never forget it.

Nine of these ladies were worship leaders and stood in front of the congregation during worship. They all wore costumes of matching colorful silk dresses that they had paid for themselves, and as the music soared, they began to dance before the Lord.

I turned around and looked at the faces of all those Filipino maids—some with tears in their eyes—singing at the top of their voices. When the service was over, they stayed in the building for hours and hours, just to be together and pray together.

What smiles! What sparkling eyes and bright voices! What great praise to our Lord ascended from that place! Yet anyone who knows how these women live would wonder how they could ever find reason to laugh or sing. From my perspective, their position in life seems little better than a slave. They work

long, long hours, six and a half days a week, endure strict regulations, and live in cramped, tiny rooms. It came to me the other day that the entire personal living area for many of these women was smaller than the bathroom off of my office in Beaverton.

I tried to imagine what one of those women might think about, when she finally lay down in her bed after a long day of work. Would the money be enough for her family? Would her husband remain faithful to her? Were the children staying out of trouble? Would they remember her, love her, miss her? Would there be any kind of life together after she returned? Yet even in the face of what must be wrenching uncertainty, these women have joy! The genuine article.

As I listened to the musical chatter of their voices in that crowded sanctuary after the service, I thought about how Paul described the believers in Macedonia—the great radiance of joy and selfless generosity arising out of deep poverty and persecution. "Though they have been going through much trouble and hard times," Paul wrote, "they have mixed their wonderful joy with their deep poverty, and the result has been an overflow of giving to others" (2 Corinthians 8:2, TLB).

Deep poverty. Great trouble. Overwhelming joy.

It's a combination that adds up only on heaven's calculator. I can remember feeling very convicted as I left the Filipino church that Sunday for the comfort of my hotel room. I said to myself, *These people have virtually nothing to be thankful for—yet they're the happiest people in the world.* I felt ashamed, but I wanted to believe that maybe God could work something of His joyous glory in my life, too, and that I wouldn't be one of those "fair weather" Christians who could only rejoice when all my circumstances were pleasant.

I really can't tell you what tomorrow holds for me. When you've had leukemia for a dozen years, you don't even try to predict. But when the chance comes for me to sing, I'm going to sing. When the chance comes for me to praise God, I'm

going to open my mouth and do it, and I won't be embarrassed.

And it's all unto Him, because He is so faithful.

Someday when we're in heaven together, when we're gathered together worshiping the Lamb of God, I think there may be, among endless surprises, a particular surprise for us. Yes, the elders will be there, casting their crowns at His feet. The cherubim and seraphim will be there, too, declaring His worthiness in ways we can't even imagine now. Choirs stretching from horizon to horizon will shout aloud with an adoration that shakes the new heavens and makes the new earth tremble. But at some moment on those occasions of glorious praise, I wouldn't be surprised to see all those redeemed saints and mighty angels step back for a moment to watch nine petite Filipino ladies in bright, swishing silk dresses approach the throne.

And then all of heaven will watch as they dance and dance their joy before the Lord of all.

1. Adapted from a story by John Ortberg in *The Life You've Always Wanted: Spiritual Disciplines for Ordinary People* (Grand Rapids, Mich.: Zondervan Publishing House, 1997), 63–5.

"Morning Is Near"

Weeping may endure for a night,
But joy comes in the morning.

PSALM 30:5

*I*t was dark, and she was all alone. Utterly desolate, she wept with no hope of consolation.

She had pinned her hope—all of it—on one Man. Stone by stone, she had rebuilt the smashed and devastated remnants of her life on His strong foundation. She owed *everything* to Him—her teacher, friend, and Lord. It was He who had delivered her from the nightmare world of demon possession. It was He who had released her from the heavy chains of habitual sin. It was His voice that had called her out of deepest darkness into a new, resplendent morning of life.

But now He was gone, it was dark, and her dreams seemed like so many ashes in her hands.

> On the first day of the week Mary Magdalene came to the tomb early, while it was still dark, and saw that the stone had been taken away from the tomb. (John 20:1–2)

Somehow, it seemed fitting that her destination was a tomb. Where else do you go when life is over and there's nothing left to believe in? She had not brought a lamp with her, and she had to feel her way along the garden path. Even from a distance, even in the heavy gloom before sunrise, she could tell that something wasn't right. A blacker, deeper darkness enveloped the spot where the stone had been only yesterday.

What had become of the body? Obviously, someone had taken it away. In a final, unthinkable indignity, someone had stolen the torn, broken remains of the Teacher and denied Mary her final act of devotion and service.

She ran for help, and John came to investigate. So did Peter. Finally, they left, shaking their heads in bewilderment. But Mary stayed on. What could she do? Where could she go? What was left for her?

Dawn, soft and pearl gray, seeped unnoticed into the eastern horizon. When she peered into the tomb and saw the two angels, she felt neither comfort nor fear. What did she care about angels? There was only One she wanted to see…and He was no more.

When a man suddenly emerged from the darkness, she wasn't even alarmed. How could anyone harm her? How could she be hurt any more profoundly than she had already been hurt?

> She turned around and saw Jesus standing there, and did not know that it was Jesus. Jesus said to her, "Woman, why are you weeping? Whom are you seeking?" She, supposing Him to be the gardener, said to Him, "Sir, if You have carried Him away, tell me where You have laid Him, and I will take Him away." (vv. 14–16)

Somebody whispered her name in the darkness.
"Mary."
But it wasn't just somebody. It was Jesus! Alive—and as

near as could be. In the darkest moment of her life, in the moment when her last hope seemed to have trickled away, He spoke her name, and just that quickly, life was worth living again.

As a pastor, I've been with people in such moments. When crushing life circumstances overwhelm you, it's really difficult to recognize the evidence of God's presence. You feel abandoned, desolate, and terribly alone. It's hard to grasp the fact that God is near at hand.

Mary had been crying so hard that she couldn't recognize the unbelievably good news right in front of her. She couldn't grasp the significance of the empty tomb. She was too heartbroken and numbed to be moved by the presence of angels. When she first saw Jesus standing there, she didn't recognize Him, either. It's hard to see much of anything when your eyes are full of tears and you're looking at the ground.

But then Jesus spoke one word—her name. And hope leaped up like a flame from a pool of lamp oil.

She hadn't recognized Him, but He recognized her! She hadn't been aware of Him in her grief and anguish, but He was aware of her. She hadn't sensed His nearness or His presence, but He knew exactly where she was and came to her. To reach Peter, Jesus had walked an impossible path across a dark and stormy sea. To reach Mary—and to reach you and me—He came right out of the grave.

Nothing, nothing, nothing, can separate Jesus Christ from those He loves.

Death can't, and life can't. The angels won't, and all the powers of hell itself cannot keep God's love away. Our fears for today, our worries about tomorrow, or where we are—high above the sky, or in the deepest ocean—nothing will ever be able to separate us from the love of God demonstrated by our Lord Jesus Christ when he died for us. (Romans 8:38–39, TLB)

In the times when I'm most discouraged and most troubled, I need to remember that even though I don't sense God, even though I can't see evidence of His presence, He is still there, and He is aware of me! He recognizes me even when I can't recognize Him or what He's doing. He knows exactly what's happening in my life and calls me by name.

When Jesus spoke Mary's name, she knew who He was—but not until that very moment.

Could He be speaking your name right now? Could He be whispering softly into your darkness? Early in the morning, Mary brought her broken heart to the tomb. Her hopes had been smashed and shattered, but still she came—to the last place she had seen Him.

And when she came, He spoke her name. She found Him alive and seeking her, even as she had sought Him. And just then, the sun came up in her life, and the shadows fled away like a bad dream.

As you read these words, you may find yourself with very little hope in your heart. You may have doubts and fears—or maybe just a big dead place in the center of your soul.

My friend, do what Mary did that Sunday morning so long ago.

Come to Jesus. Come with all your heartaches and fears. Come with your sin and your enslaving habits. Come with your disappointments and cynicism and doubts. Come to Him just as you are and as best you know how.

Then listen.

That whisper you hear in the dark is the voice of God's Son. He is speaking your name. He is seeking you at the same time you are seeking Him. He is alive. He is awake. He is at work. And He has been watching over your life all along, even when you were unaware of His presence.

It's been dark in your life long enough, hasn't it?

Step into the sunrise of God's love.

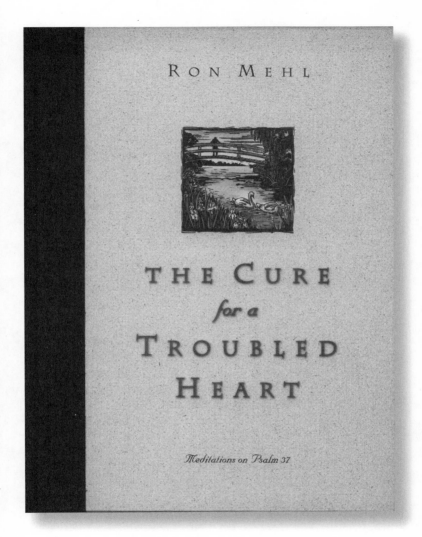

RON MEHL

THE CURE
for a
TROUBLED
HEART

Meditations on Psalm 37

Based on verses from Psalm 37, this book contains reflective, poignant meditations that reveal God's deep love and care for us. They encourage readers to respond to who God is...and delight in His response.

ISBN 1-57673-017-4

Twenty-Five Acts of Love Your Father Performs for You While You Sleep

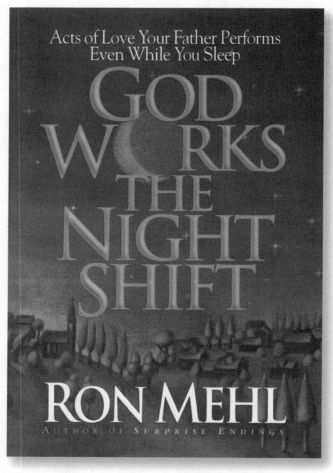

Sometimes we feel that God is working by leaps and bounds in the lives of others, but not in our own. Especially when we are going through difficult times, it may seem as though other people have been richly blessed—while our own lives are completely empty. But Ron Mehl assures you that despite the way things sometimes appear, God is continually at work in your life. He often does His best works in the darkness. Take a closer look at the God who works the night shift, and learn about the unceasing acts of love He performs for you, every moment of your life...even while you sleep.

ISBN 0-88070-718-6

GOD'S LOVE SHINES BRIGHTEST WHEN YOU NEED IT MOST

Facing the day-to-day challenges of life, it's easy to convince ourselves we can solve any crisis. Sometimes it takes a dead end to remind us that we don't have all the answers—but God does. Through a series of inspiring true-life stories—some gripping, others hilarious—Ron Mehl illustrates how dead ends in life can make us reach for God with a sincerity and eagerness we have never known before. God can transform any dead end into a highway of triumph over disappointment and a mighty assurance of His love.

ISBN 1-57673-339-4

THERE IS PURPOSE FOR YOUR PAIN

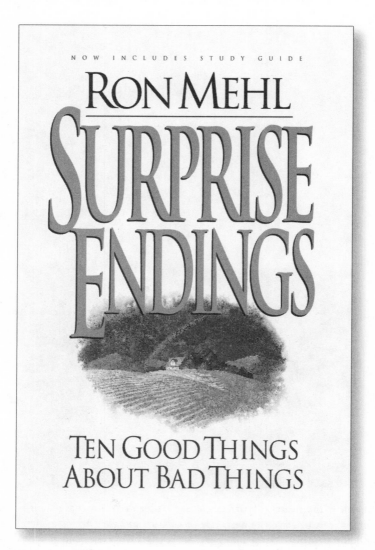

NOW INCLUDES STUDY GUIDE

RON MEHL

SURPRISE ENDINGS

TEN GOOD THINGS ABOUT BAD THINGS

For every reader who has ever wondered whether God sees their suffering...for those who wonder if there is any purpose for their pain...for those who wonder why God allows their struggles to continue. Ron Mehl weaves personal stories with Scripture, offers wise insights on loneliness, death, hard choices, failure, and other challenges, and guides us toward victory in Christ.

ISBN 1-88070-828-X

A Dad's Counsel to a Son or Daughter Leaving Home

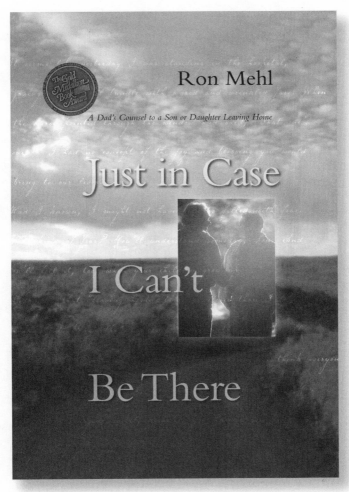

This book is the heart-to-heart talk every father desires to have with a son or daughter about to leave the nest. *Just in Case I Can't Be There* is a friendly chat around the campfire. In a manner that is wise, winsome, and practical, best-selling author and pastor Ron Mehl offers godly, biblical counsel in thirty-four concise, entertaining chapters. Dealing with diverse issues about faith and integrity ranging from choosing a mate to managing finances, the wisdom contained in these pages will offer encouragement, boost confidence, and provide guidance for years to come. This is the one book that no young person should be without.

ISBN 1-57673-542-7

COMFORT AND HOPE FOR LIFE'S MOST DIFFICULT MOMENTS

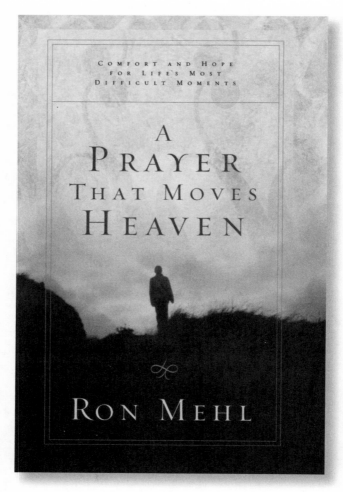

Beginning with one of the most dramatic, triumphant stories of God's deliverance in all of Scripture, beloved pastor and author Dr. Ron Mehl describes the kind of prayer—and the kind of life—that moves heaven. Rich with stories and principles from twenty-five years of ministry, the book shows how to prepare for moments of deep life crisis, and how to pray when the storms roar in from out of nowhere. King Jehoshaphat had no defense and no plan when a surprise invasion came upon Jerusalem—and that's the moment when he discovered resources and power beyond his imagination.

ISBN 1-57673-885-X

CONFINING RULES,
OR STATEMENTS OF GOD'S LOVE?

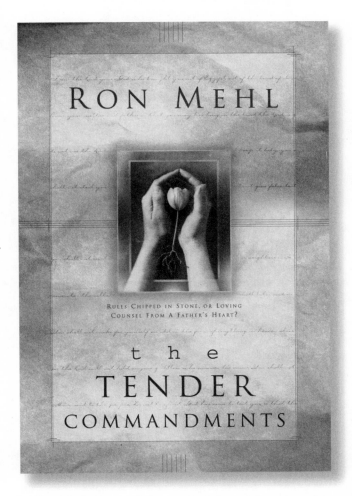

The ten Commandments are often portrayed as ominous warnings—cold, harsh words from an all-powerful and vengeful God. This book recasts them as messages of love—ten declarations of our Creator's love for us. Pastor and award-winning author Ron Mehl interprets the ten Commandments as guiding steps that can keep us from being bruised and broken by the deadly traps of a fallen world. He shows how, rather than running into the same brick walls of life, clawing helplessly up the same impassable sand banks, we can be led by God's guiding hand and walk through life with confidence.

ISBN 1-57673-772-2

DATE DUE
